SUNSHINE
from the
LATTER-DAY
SAINT
CHILD'S
SOUL

SUNSHINE
from the
LATTER-DAY
SAINT
CHILD'S
SOUL

EAGLE GATE

SALT LAKE CITY, UTAH

Library of Congress Cataloging-in-Publication Data

Sunshine from the Latter-day Saint child's soul.
    p. cm.
ISBN 1-57345-924-0 (pbk.)
   1. Children—Religious life. 2. Christian life—Mormon authors.
I. Deseret Book Company.

BX8643.C56 S86 2001
242'.62—dc21

00-066313

Printed in the United States of America   54459-6795

10 9   8   7   6   5   4   3   2   1

Contents

Preface xi

Happiness and Humor

- Seven Little Boys 3
  SPENCER W. KIMBALL
- A Bad Day? 5
  KENNETH L. HARVEY
- Four Friends 6
  ASHBY MINER
- Wrong, but Not Far Off 7
  PAUL BOUCHARD
- Single White Male, Primary Teacher 9
  MICHAELENE P. GRASSLI
- Listening to the Bishop 11
  JEFF SCHRADE
- A Cure for Anger 12
  LINDA J. EYRE
- A Reverent Mouth 13
  ANDY MENOUGH
- "You Did Real Good, Honey" 14
  LYNDA RAE AND LEONARD MARDEN
- A Tough Interview with the Bishop 15
  LOIS CARTER
- Two Kind Deeds? 17
  MICHAELENE P. GRASSLI

Family

- The Faith of a Little Child 21
  TAMRA CHRISTENSEN
- The Upgrade 23
  ROBERT FARRELL SMITH
- "Look Who's Here!" 25
  BARBARA B. SMITH
- Source of Income 26
  SHANE ADAMSON

- Two Fathers 27
  ERIC KNIGHT
- Dad Can Fix It 28
  W. TIMOTHY HILL
- Little Arms of Comfort 30
  LISA J. PECK
- Family First 32
  PAUL COX
- Sister Mom and Elder Dad 34
  MICHAELENE P. GRASSLI

Scriptures

- "Peace, Be Still" 37
  KRISTEN HUDSON
- Sacred Scrolls 39
  MICKIE MORTENSEN ORTIZ
- The Thirteenth Article of Faith 40
  TERRY ALDERMAN
- The Book of Mormon and *The Cat in the Hat* 42
  JULIE SESSIONS
- "That's Not How It Goes!" 44
  STEFENEE HYMAS
- Joshua and President Kimball 45
  BARBARA B. SMITH
- "Heinous, Heinous, Yay!" 47
  KIMBERLY OTTOSEN

Holidays

- A Children's Play 51
  ANONYMOUS
- The Truth about the Easter Bunny 53
  BARBARA B. SMITH
- The Anonymous Benefactor 54
  SUSAN EASTON BLACK
- Faith in Christ 59
  MIGNON COLEY
- An Easter Egg Hunt 60
  L. E. JACOBSEN

- A Teacher's Christmas 62
  BRAD WILCOX
- A Magical Christmas 64
  RICHARD PETERSON

Heaven and Deity

- The Most Important Thing 69
  F. ENZIO BUSCHE
- "More Room in Heaven" 72
  LESLIE JENSEN
- Heavenly Father Knows 73
  AUTHOR UNKNOWN
- A Young Admirer 75
  PETER B. GARDNER
- A Voice of Warning 76
  HAROLD B. LEE
- Which One Was He? 77
  JULIE STEINBERG
- The Purity of a Child 78
  DEAN WESSENDORF
- The Most Influential People 80
  SHONNA C. DODSON
- A Child's Testimony 82
  SHANE DIXON
- Words of Wisdom 85
  MONTY HAYS

A Child's Perspective

- The Simple Pleasures of Childhood 89
  JANENE WOLSEY BAADSGAARD
- The Good Food 92
  NONA L. BRADY
- "Poor, Yet Possessing All Things" 94
  JOYCE BAGGERLY
- Reverently, Quietly 99
  SUSAN A. SANDBERG
- "What Makes You Have a Bad Day?" 101
  MARSHA ROSE STEED
- Blessings for Eva 103
  PETER B. GARDNER

- "My Body *Is* the Happy" 105
  LINDA J. AND RICHARD EYRE
- Authority to Baptize 107
  M. KATHERINE EDWARDS
- Spilt Milk 109
  CHAR GWYN
- The Grand Amen 110
  VALERIE BUCK

Faith, Courage, and Determination

- "I Will Have My Father . . . Hold Me in His Arms" 117
  LUCY MACK SMITH
- Ballad of the Tempest 121
  JAMES THOMAS FIELDS
- Bricks or Straw? 123
  ARDETH GREENE KAPP
- "What If You Die, Mom?" 126
  DANIEL QUILLEN
- "Throw It Here, Sissy!" 128
  HEBER J. GRANT
- "He Blessed Me That I Might Be Healed" 130
  GEORGE ALBERT SMITH
- Fasting for Grandma 132
  WILMA AEBISCHER
- Saving the Book of Commandments 134
  MARY ELIZABETH ROLLINS LIGHTNER

Gospel Principles

- The Building Fund Goat 139
  ELDON ROSS PALMER
- Wash Away Sins 144
  KENT STEPHENS
- It's Sometimes Hard to Say No 145
  STEPHANIE JENSON
- Heidi Loves the Sacrament 146
  BECKY W. KEARL
- I'll Soon Be Eight 148
  GENEVA FACEMYER

- I Love to See the Temple 149
  FIONA HOWELL
- The Confession 151
  MEL JONES
- "You Don't Have the Priesthood Yet" 154
  YOLANDA DIXON
- Giving Credit Where Credit Is Due 155
  MARSHA HUGHES

Birth, Death, and Resurrection

- To Live with Father in Heaven 159
  ROD BOSS
- Born Here 161
  BRAD WILCOX
- Repairing Grandpa 162
  ROBERT P. BARNES
- The Age of a Tree 164
  LORI SMITH
- Burying Fred 165
  ELYSSA RENEE ANDRUS
- A Potato Bug Reunion 170
  MICHAELENE P. GRASSLI
- Simple Faith 171
  JULIANN DOMAN
- The Will of the Lord 173
  MARBA C. JOSEPHSON

Prayer

- "Nothing Will Hurt You" 177
  DAVID O. MCKAY
- An Unusual Answer 179
  LINDA TENNEY
- "How About Your Prayers?" 181
  ROBERT L. SIMPSON
- "Doctor, Won't You Pray for Me?" 182
  GEORGE ALBERT SMITH
- "But What Should I Say, Daddy?" 184
  RON MATHES
- "For of Such Is the Kingdom of God" 185
  CINDY COLLYER

- A Prayer for Bobby 187
  MICHAELENE P. GRASSLI
- "And Please Bless . . ." 188
  MATTHEW O. RICHARDSON
- A Sister in a Storm 190
  KATHY FORD
- Michael's Prayer 192
  MICHAELENE P. GRASSLI
- "The Wind Has Gone Down!" 193
  SOPHY H. VALENTINE
- Faith of a Child 196
  HEBER C. KIMBALL

Love and Service

- Love Thy Neighbor 199
  ARDETH GREENE KAPP
- "I Didn't Want You to Be Alone" 201
  MICHAELENE P. GRASSLI
- "Daddy, Why Do You Love Me?" 202
  SCOTT SATTERFIELD
- Angels in Camouflage 204
  CORINA BURNER
- "Because He Loved Them" 206
  SHANE DIXON
- Pacified 210
  LINDA J. EYRE
- The Mean Man Next Door 211
  ANGIE OLSON
- Friends for Andre 213
  MICHAELENE P. GRASSLI
- Ears to Hear 215
  PAULA HUNT
- A Turf War Averted 217
  BARBARA B. SMITH

Sources and Permissions 219

Preface

At the same time came the disciples
unto Jesus, saying, Who is the greatest in
the kingdom of heaven?

And Jesus called a little child unto him,
and set him in the midst of them,

And said, Verily I say unto you, Except
ye be converted, and become as little children, ye shall not enter into the kingdom
of heaven.

Whosoever therefore shall humble himself as this little child, the same is greatest
in the kingdom of heaven. (Matthew
18:1–4)

What is it about children that would cause Jesus to
set them up as examples for adults to follow? Perhaps it
is children's unquestioning faith in their parents and in
God, a faith that is often lost in our struggle for independence and maturity. Or maybe it is children's guile-
less nature, seen in their simple, often humorous,

approach to life's complexities and difficulties. Or maybe it is because children, who know of their own weakness and lack of understanding, are ever ready to learn and grow from all of life's lessons. These and many other qualities make children apt models for grown-ups to follow as they reexamine their lives.

Sunshine from the Latter-day Saint Child's Soul offers grown-up readers 101 lessons in being childlike. These stories reflect the joy of discovery and the humor inherent in children's attempts to make sense of this sometimes strange and overly complex world. Along with accounts of the lighter side of childhood are stories that tell of children's ability to be "submissive, meek, humble, patient, [and] full of love" (Mosiah 3:19). Children's quickness to forgive, slowness to judge, and easiness to love all come out in these heart-warming stories.

With selections from such beloved authors as Michaelene P. Grassli, Barbara B. Smith, Matthew O. Richardson, Brad Wilcox, Shane Dixon, Linda J. and Richard Eyre, and Robert Farrell Smith, *Sunshine from the Latter-day Saint Child's Soul* will help readers see life as they once saw it, full of wonder, possibility, and the love of Heavenly Father.

The publisher thanks the many authors whose stories are included in this volume, as well as Brad Wilcox and Shane Dixon, who compiled the bulk of the stories; Mindy Gandolph and Tamara Grandstaff, who did preliminary editing; Debbie Bright, Laura Campbell, James

Melton, Fara Sneddon, Janet Titensor, Jill Taylor, and Patricia Carrington, who helped revise the manuscript; Dave Crockett and Dave Kenison at LDSWorld-Gems (ldsworld.com), who allowed the compilers to tap into their resources; and Randi Johansen, who helped with the book's concept. Special thanks to Chris Crowe and John Bennion.

Happiness
and
Humor

Seven Little Boys

SPENCER W. KIMBALL

Long years ago when I was in the presidency of the St. Joseph Stake in Arizona, one Sabbath day I filled an assignment in the Eden Ward. The building was a small one, and most of the people were close to us as we sat on the raised platform about a foot and a half above the floor of the building itself.

As the meeting proceeded, my eye was attracted to seven little boys on the front seat of the chapel. I was delighted that they were in this ward conference. I made a mental note, then shifted my interest to other things. Soon my attention was focused on the seven little boys again.

It seemed strange to me that each of the seven raised his right leg and put it over the left knee, and then in a moment all would change at the same time and put the left leg over the right knee. I thought it was unusual, but I just ignored it.

In a moment or two, all in unison brushed their hair with their right hands; then all seven boys leaned lightly on their wrists and supported their faces by their hands, and then simultaneously they went back to crossing their legs again.

It all seemed so strange, and I wondered about it as I was trying to think of what I was going to say in the meeting. And then suddenly it came to me like a bolt of lightning: These boys were mimicking me!

That day I learned the lesson of my life—that we who are in positions of authority must be careful indeed, because others watch us and find in us their examples.

I accompanied Russell to the priesthood preview meeting at the stake center. We arrived a little early, and no one was in the chapel. Russell said, "Wow Dad! Is this what the church looks like when you're on time?"

—Brad Wilcox

A Bad Day?

KENNETH L. HARVEY

An incident I observed during a visit to my daughter's home involves having a good attitude, an important trait we look for in our youth today. My ten-year-old grandson had just returned from school, and his mother noticed that his legs, arms, and the front of his jacket were wet and muddy. His mother asked him what had happened. The boy replied that, while he was waiting for the bus, an upper-grade boy came up behind him and gave him a shove, causing him to fall headlong onto the wet ground.

His mother said, "I'm sorry that you had such a bad day!"

"I didn't have a bad day!" the boy replied. "I had a wonderful day. I just had a bad few minutes."

Four Friends

ASHBY MINER, AGE SEVEN

Sleeping Beauty went to Jasmine's castle. She wanted to be friends. Jasmine liked Sleeping Beauty, and she said, "I have a cousin, and she is coming tomorrow. Do you want to meet her?"

"Oh yes," said Sleeping Beauty.

"Her name is Belle," said Jasmine. Belle came. She was beautiful.

"Do you want to meet another friend?" asked Belle.

"Yes," said the other girls. Then Cinderella came in.

Then Aladdin and the Beast and Prince Phillip and the other handsome prince came. "We want to play," they said.

"No way!" said the girls.

And the four girls lived happily ever after in Jasmine's castle. And the four boys cried their guts out.

Wrong, but Not Far Off

PAUL BOUCHARD

Several years ago, back when Primary classes had names like Sunbeam, Star A and B, CTR A and B, Valiant A and B, and so on, I was asked by the Primary president to substitute a class composed of a particularly wild bunch of seven- and eight-year-old boys. It turns out that the president was having a hard time finding a permanent teacher for this class.

The next week there still wasn't an official teacher found to instruct the class, and the Primary president asked if I would mind teaching again. I told her I would be happy to teach and let her know that I enjoyed this group of boys (probably because I was a little bit like them when I was a lad). After the same thing happened for two more weeks, I was finally called to be the permanent teacher of the class. I gladly accepted and had a wonderful year with those boys.

As we neared the end of the year and the boys were

preparing to move to the Valiant B class, a boy named Kevin turned to me in the middle of Primary and said, "Brother Bouchard, just think, in a couple more weeks we'll be Violent Bs."

Sister Wilson carefully studied each young child as she entered the Primary classroom. *How they have grown and developed since January,* she thought. She gathered them around her and began her lesson. "You are each very special! You have learned so many things. You have learned to sit reverently and listen to our lessons. Why, you can even say your own prayers!"

"Well, of course," responded Clayton, "I've been on this earth five years!"

—Ruth B. Wright

From *Best-Loved Humor of the LDS People,* ed. Linda Ririe Gundry, Jay A. Parry, and Jack M. Lyon, 220–21.

Single White Male, Primary Teacher

MICHAELENE P. GRASSLI

Two little girls were in Primary opening exercises when an announcement was made reminding teachers of the ward adult Valentine party. The leader making the announcement specifically addressed the girls' teacher, a young, single, recently returned missionary. He was encouraged to get a date and attend. The young man commented that he probably would not attend because he didn't think he could get a date.

The two little girls, much concerned for their teacher, decided to do something about his dateless situation. They went to his home when he wasn't there and got a picture of him from his family. They glued it to a poster on which they wrote, "Will you go out with me?" Then they took it to a young adult ward in the area, stood in the foyer with a clipboard and pencil, and stopped likely looking girls. In a few minutes they had several names. When they took the poster and list back to their teacher's house, he was mortified! But the girls, insistent, pointed out the names of the young adult women they thought had the most potential. Their teacher went to the Valentine party with a date recruited by his Primary girls!

When my nineteen-year-old daughter was about three, I asked her when she was going to get married. She said she never would. I asked why she would say that. She replied, "Because I asked all the boys, and they said no."

—Ann Workman

Listening to the Bishop

JEFF SCHRADE

It was a hot, sultry August day, and the heat in our little chapel was rising. The doors were propped open for ventilation, but the effect was minimal. The bishop was doing his best to convey a deep doctrinal message, but the heat was beginning to win over converts, and more than a few souls had already nodded off to the pleasures of the unconscious state. Finally my four-year-old couldn't take it anymore. She climbed up onto my lap, threw her arms around my neck, closed her eyes, and said: "When the bishop says one or two things, that's okay, but when he says five or six things, he just puts me right to sleep."

Everyone around me laughed, and several smiled in agreement.

A Cure for Anger
LINDA J. EYRE

One night at bedtime, I remember being absolutely furious with our four-year-old, who had pushed me to the edge. I grabbed him by the shoulders and started to shake him and scold him vehemently. Suddenly he looked in my face and let out a peal of laughter. It made me even more angry to think he would laugh in the face of such wrath, and I was outraged! After another peal of laughter, I finally blared out, "What are you laughing about?"

"Mommy, you look so funny," he roared. And his little brother in the other bed, who had been looking on with unbelief, started to laugh too. I thought for a minute about how ridiculous I must look, and then (though I tried not to) I broke up too. Soon the other children heard us laughing and came running in to find out why. None of us could even explain. We just laughed until our sides hurt.

A Reverent Mouth

ANDY MENOUGH

During the Primary sharing time, my friend was teaching the children what it means to be reverent. She had taken the time to draw the different body parts to help the younger children understand.

As sharing time began, she stood and held up the different cards. As she held them up, she would ask such questions as "What do you do with your arms?" And the children would answer, "Fold them."

As she held up the drawing of the mouth, she asked the children, "What do you do with your mouths?"

One small child in the Sunbeam class quickly responded, "Kiss!"

"You Did Real Good, Honey"

LYNDA RAE AND LEONARD MARDEN

Our four-year-old nephew, Willie, was involved in the Primary presentation in sacrament meeting. During the practices for the presentation he had listened to all of the children in his class rehearse their parts, so he knew what everyone was supposed to say.

During the meeting the little girl next to Willie froze up and could not do her part. Willie put his arm around her and coached her through her lines. After she was finished, he patted her arm and said, "You did real good, honey."

The whole congregation laughed, and Willie just smiled and sat down.

A Tough Interview
with the Bishop

LOIS CARTER

When my granddaughter Brittany turned eight years old, her dad and mom took her for an interview with the bishop in preparation for baptism. Her father, who had once served as bishop, told her some of the questions the bishop would ask her in the interview.

When they arrived at the church, the bishop called her into his office, leaving her mom and dad in the foyer. It wasn't long before the bishop came to the door and called for her dad. He said that they needed his help, as Brittany was having trouble remembering her birthday. Her father went in, and in a short time they finished the interview and were on their way home.

As they were leaving the church, her dad asked, "Brittany, don't you know when your birthday is?"

Brittany answered, "Yes, I do. It's July 10, 1989. But he didn't ask me when my birthday was; he asked me if I remembered when I was born, and I told him no!"

During a Primary lesson on the bishopric, the teacher asked the children what a bishop does. Without hesitation, a bright six-year-old answered, "Moves diagonally."

—Anonymous

A few weeks after being called as bishop, I brought my family into the bishop's office for tithing settlement. Hoping to share with my children some of the duties I now performed, I explained that this was the office where I now conducted various meetings and interviews. My five-year-old son surveyed the office and, spotting a photograph of President Hinckley hanging on the wall, said, "I see President Hinckley used to work here."

—Nolan Larsen

Two Kind Deeds?

MICHAELENE P. GRASSLI

One day, when [five-year-old Ulrike's] father asked her why she looked so unhappy, she confided that she didn't like going to kindergarten. It turned out that a larger girl at school frequently pushed and kicked her.

Her father took this opportune moment to explain about loving our enemies. He challenged his little girl to answer each unkind deed with two kind deeds. That way she and her good deeds would always be victorious, because the kindness would outweigh the unkindness. They prayed together and her father was certain his daughter had learned a masterful lesson.

In a few days the father noticed that Ulrike's demeanor had improved, so he asked about the problem they'd discussed.

"Oh, she doesn't come to kindergarten anymore. My prayer was answered."

"And did you try the two kind deeds for each unkindness?"

"Yes. Once when she kicked me, I gave her two candies." Then, with a triumphant sparkle in her eyes, Ulrike added, "So her teeth will rot!"

Russell was bored and said, "Mom, I'm not having no fun."

Mom corrected, "I'm not having any fun."

Russell said, "Well I'm not either!"

—Brad Wilcox

18

Family

The Faith of a Little Child

TAMRA CHRISTENSEN

Out of school for the summer, my three boys were racing in and out of the house while I chased after their two-year-old sister, Sarah, who was doing her best to keep up with them. Desperately needing to get some housework done, I asked my oldest son, Jason, if he would watch her, which he reluctantly agreed to do.

A little while later, Jason came walking into the kitchen to find something to eat. Realizing he was alone, I asked him, "Where's Sarah?"

Looking at me as if I were questioning his ability to keep track of her, he sarcastically said, "Oh, she's out playing in the street."

Even though I knew he wasn't serious, I let out a sigh of relief when I heard her singing softly as she walked up the stairs from our basement. My five-year-old son, Adam, however, overheard Jason's remark but apparently didn't know that Sarah really was in the house.

Suddenly, with a worried look on his face, he jumped off the couch and ran out to search for his little sister.

From our front window I could see him frantically running up and down the street, calling, "Sarah, Sarah!"

As I opened the door to call for Adam, what I saw touched my heart. There was my little boy kneeling on the sidewalk with his head bowed and his hands clasped together. I could see his lips moving as he quietly prayed for help to find Sarah.

Gratitude welled up inside me as I saw the love Adam had for his little sister! Seeing him there on his knees, oblivious to the cars whizzing by, I knew that, had Sarah actually been lost, Heavenly Father would have answered his prayer. And from Adam's point of view, He did.

As I was looking ahead to my husband's going out of town for a week, leaving me alone with our four children, I indicated that I'd like my mom to come "tend us." The children had even a better idea—we could go tend Grandma, who lived some 450 miles away. I told them not to tempt me more than I could withstand, to which four little voices chorused, "Tempt! Tempt! Tempt!"
—Rebecca Chambers

The Upgrade

ROBERT FARRELL SMITH

Recently I had the opportunity to take my seven-year-old daughter, Kindred, with me on a business trip to Seattle, Washington. After arriving at the Seattle airport, we made our way over to the car rental place to pick up our car. Having never been really all that cool and being accustomed to driving a minivan, I had visions of renting a car that might up my "cool index" for the few days we would be there. I told the woman at the desk I wanted something fast with leather seats and a nice stereo—maybe even a convertible. As she was looking up my request, I leaned over to Kindred and asked her what features she wanted our car to have. She looked up at me and said, "Could we get one without air bags so that I can sit by you?"

We spent the next fifteen minutes begging the car rental woman to find us the oldest, most outdated car she could possibly locate so that my daughter could safely ride next to me in the front seat. After all, I really couldn't think of a finer feature for the car than family.

Grandpa took little Wendee to see the Christmas program at the local elementary school. When they got home I asked, "Did you see candy canes? ornaments? lights?" After each item she nodded vigorously. "Which did you like best?" I asked.

Without hesitation she responded, "Grandpa!"
—Brad Wilcox

"Look Who's Here!"

BARBARA B. SMITH

Some years ago when one of my daughters was a small, exuberant child we were all sitting around the fireplace as families do at the happy Christmas season. . . . Fathers, mothers, cousins, aunts, and uncles all chatted quietly by the fire, and into this large group of people who loved each other bounded my child with the exclamation, "Look who's here, everybody!"

Our curiosity was piqued by this enthusiastic announcement. We looked beyond her with interest and inquired, "Who is it?"

And she returned our questioning glances with sparkling eyes and a face wreathed in smiles and announced, "Me!"

It was not what we had expected, somehow, but I shall never forget that moment. This little bit of a girl taught her older kinfolk an important lesson.

Source of Income

SHANE ADAMSON

When our family went to the Barnum and Bailey Circus, the tickets seemed overpriced, so we bought just one cotton candy for all of us to share. It included some clown glasses. But my son Taylor had seen other kids with big, bright elephant lights and said he didn't want the glasses. He begged and begged for me to buy the light but with no success.

After the performance when we were putting Taylor in his car seat, he pouted, "Let's not go home yet!"

"Where would you like to go, Taylor?" we asked.

"Let's go to Toys "R" Us and get elephant light!"

"Taylor," I asked, "do you have any money?"

"Yes, I do!"

Surprised, I questioned, "Where is your money?"

He quickly responded, "It's in your pocket."

Two Fathers

ERIC KNIGHT

When my stepdaughter, Samantha, was six years old and was going through a difficult interval dealing with her parents' divorce, we would talk with her as much as she wanted to help her get through it. When she finally seemed to be perfectly happy again, I asked how she was dealing with it. She replied, "It's okay—Jesus had two daddies, too." Although neither of her fathers comes anywhere near the level of Jesus' "daddies," it was comforting to her to know that Jesus was raised by his stepfather, just as she was.

Dad Can Fix It

W. TIMOTHY HILL

Many years ago one of my young sons taught me an important lesson. My son was only four at the time, and one of his favorite pastimes was going on rides in the car with his grandma. One of the reasons he liked the rides so much is that Grandma's car was a vintage Volkswagen Beetle. They would get in, roll all the windows down, and sail down the road, munching on Snickers candy bars and letting their hair blow in the breeze.

On one particular day, they were riding along and my son knelt on the seat so he could stick his head out the window.

His grandmother quickly said to him, "Cameron, get your head back inside the car. We might go by a building or telephone pole or something, and it would take your head right off."

My son looked at his grandmother and confidently

replied, "It wouldn't matter if my head came off, because my dad could put it back on again."

When my mother related the story to the family, we all laughed. But I was also humbled by the faith that this young boy had in his father. He wasn't trying to be funny. He really believed that his dad could fix it. I thought of my Heavenly Father and realized that this is the faith and confidence I should have in him. Cameron taught me a great lesson that day. I have strived since that time to be a father deserving of that kind of faith.

An LDS child needed to bring an old shirt from home for a school project about drug prevention. The mother was busy and handed her child an old T-shirt without examining it. Later, she was appalled to see her child wearing the T-shirt through the mall. On the front it said, "A Family Is Forever." On the back it read, "Be Smart, Don't Start."

—Abraham Miller

Little Arms of Comfort
LISA J. PECK

Sometimes it feels like a hailstorm of trials are upon us.

The year 1993 was such a time for me. The first storm came with the untimely end of a much-wanted pregnancy after twelve weeks of acute nausea. I mourned this loss and grew more grateful for my short, stocky, auburn-haired son. He seemed to understand my need for comfort and would give me quick kisses before he rushed off to play with his toys.

Several other crises added to my misery, and I found myself often in need of comfort. One day I was sitting on the floor and crying, almost as if I were the child in need of a parent.

My son heard my sobs. He rushed into the hall, running to me. Too caught up in my tears, I didn't look up.

"It's okay, Mommy," he said and then wrapped his arms as far as they would extend around me.

Hugging him back, I felt the soft thud of his heartbeat on my shoulder. As I continued to cry, he slumped down onto his knees, still hanging onto me.

When I finished, I loosened my grasp on him and said, "Thank you."

He didn't move, just continued to hug. Thinking it very odd for him to stay still for any amount of time, I gently pushed him from me to discover that he had fallen asleep on his knees while comforting his mother.

I felt a little perturbed after reminding my four-year-old daughter for the fifth time to put her book on the shelf. She, however, handled the situation beautifully. She snuggled up to me, batted her eyelashes, and said, "Please don't fire me, Mom."

—Bridgette Little

Family First

PAUL COX

As the bishop of our ward in Rome, New York, I've experienced some growing pains along with the many blessings that have come with the call. One time I got after my eleven-year-old daughter for having tried to interrupt me while a member of our ward was talking to me the previous Sunday. I told her that she should wait until I was finished talking before asking me for something.

"But Daddy," she said, "you don't make other people wait if you're talking to us and they ask to talk with you. You tell us to hold on for a second and start talking with them."

Humbled by her response, I replied, "You're right. I apologize."

I was counseled at the time of my calling to remember my family and put them first. This experience showed me how easy it is to stray off that course. But thanks to my sweet daughter and the great counsel she gave me, I have come to realize that, even though I am considered the father of the ward, I have three awesome kids, and I am their father first.

While riding in the car with my wife, our two young daughters (ages five and three) began fighting. When their mother said to the oldest, "Oh, don't teach her how to hit," she replied, "She already knows how to hit."

—Richard Peterson

I hadn't shaved before kissing my three-year-old son, David. He quickly pulled away and complained, "Dad, your freckles are sharp!"

—Brad Wilcox

Sister Mom and Elder Dad

MICHAELENE P. GRASSLI

Four-year-old Michael asked his friend as they were playing, "Will you miss me when I go on my mission?"

The friend's mother was nearby and had overheard. "Are you going on a mission, Michael?" she asked.

"Yep!"

"Won't you miss your mommy and daddy?"

"Oh," he replied confidently, "they're going with me."

Scriptures

"Peace, Be Still"

KRISTEN HUDSON

In our ward my son Mitchell has a fantastic Primary teacher named Brother Melendez. Brother Melendez puts a lot of time and energy into his lessons to help his five-year-old students understand the gospel and the stories of the scriptures. One Sunday they had a lesson about the power of the priesthood, which particularly impressed my son. Mitchell was excited to learn that someday he, too, would have this power. I am sure many examples and stories of priesthood power were discussed in Brother Melendez's lesson. It was Mitchell's application of one of these scriptural stories that caught my attention.

At the end of a particularly difficult day, my three energetic children were getting to be a little much for me. My patience was nearly depleted when I caught Mitchell doing something that he knew would upset me. When he saw me looking at him, the expression on my face said it all—he knew he was busted. I didn't speak for a moment. It took all my remaining patience to handle this disobedience appropriately.

As the anger expressed in my face deepened, he counseled with an elongated pronunciation, "Beeeee caaaalm."

Of course this sort of tutelage from a five-year-old only succeeded in increasing my swelling rage. But before I could get started with my tirade, he courageously and piously faced me with all the faith of a child, raised both arms in the air, and gently but firmly proclaimed, "Peace, be still!"

I couldn't believe what I was hearing. All traces of anger immediately left me as I stood in dumbfounded amusement at my little man. I guess he thought that if Jesus could calm the angry seas by such an utterance, the phrase might also work on an angry mother. And in its own way, it did! Not that there wasn't a "talking to" forthcoming, but Mitchell's antics drove the spirit of anger out of me, and I was able to resume my motherly duties.

Sacred Scrolls

MICKIE MORTENSEN ORTIZ

While serving in the stake Relief Society presidency, I was asked to substitute for the Sunbeam class in Primary. It was delightful and renewing to be with the pure children.

During sharing time the Primary president was talking about the sacred scrolls (the scriptures) and had two scrolls to demonstrate the stick of Judah and the stick of Joseph. She asked if anyone had ever seen sacred scrolls before.

Susie Wilkinson was sitting on my lap and could hardly contain herself as she waved her hand to get the Primary president's attention. When she was finally called on, Susie promptly replied, "I have seen scrolls (squirrels) and chickmunks (chipmunks)!"

It was all I could do to keep from laughing out loud. I love Relief Society, but you just don't get those kinds of answers from the adults! Children are great!

The Thirteenth Article of Faith

TERRY ALDERMAN

Our family has a regular learning time every morning during the summer to keep our minds active and on good things. We always have a theme—this year it was the thirteenth article of faith. Each morning we would start with prayer, do a half hour of scripture study, and then recite the thirteenth article of faith from a poster.

During study time our four-year-old could not seem to sit still. Fearful that I'd lose the attention of the older children, I let her wander about the kitchen, dining room, and living room as we studied. About a month into the summer and to the amazement of the entire family, as we started to recite the article of faith, she stopped in the kitchen doorway and said it with us, word for word. We coaxed her into the living room and had her do it on her own. It wasn't perfect, but it was close enough. By the end of the summer she had it down pat.

This reaffirmed to me the blessings of scripture study and also demonstrated how much a child can learn as a family lives the commandments given to us by a living prophet. It also reaffirmed to me the importance of monitoring what our children learn from the television, videos, radio, school, and day-care centers. They are learning every minute from whatever is there before them, good or bad.

But there is more to this story. Toward the end of the summer it was her turn to give a talk in Primary. Together we decided she would recite the thirteenth article of faith. She did, word for word. The Blazers on the back row nearly fell off their chairs in amazement. "Wow, did you hear that?" Her talk was a big hit.

My little son and daughter (ages two and three, respectively) were playing in the backyard just below our kitchen window. Arthur turned to his sister and said, "Marie, you be the nurse, and I'll be Dr. Covenants!"

—Sherry Adcock

The Book of Mormon and
The Cat in the Hat

JULIE SESSIONS

This story is not profound or funny. It is a simple illustration of the special spirits that Heavenly Father is sending to the earth today. It is also a reminder that it is never too early to teach our children gospel principles.

The other night as I was putting the baby to sleep, I asked our two-year-old son to pick out some of his favorite bedtime stories for me to read to him. When I went into his room, I immediately recognized *Danny and the Dinosaur, If You Give a Pig a Pancake,* and *The Cat in the Hat.* I also noticed that he had taken the Book of Mormon off the shelf. Before I could say anything, my sweet little boy said, "I got some books. Will you read the scriptures first?" I was so touched that he wanted to read the scriptures first that I could hardly read for a few minutes. After we finished reading, we talked about how much Jesus loves him. He wanted to read only one other book after that. He was "filled," and he closed his eyes with a big smile on his face. I felt the Spirit so strongly in his little bedroom that night.

I feel like the special spirits that are being sent to the earth right now are yearning to feel the Spirit and learn truth and righteousness. It is our joy and responsibility to teach them and learn from them.

> We were reading scriptures, and Russell was amazed at how old Adam and the other Old Testament prophets lived to be. He said in all seriousness, "If they lived to be 900, I wonder how old they had to be to drive."
>
> —Brad Wilcox

"That's Not How It Goes!"

STEFENEE HYMAS

We began reading the scriptures together as a New Year's resolution. At the time, the kids were one, three, and five. The resolution was harder to keep than we thought it would be. The kids had a hard time sitting still and didn't seem to be paying any attention. We questioned whether anyone was getting anything out of it. Then one day we had a confirmation that the kids were learning from our scripture study.

Stevie, the three-year-old, asked me to read him a story. I told him to choose the book he wanted read. He brought me the book, and I began to read, "Once upon a time . . ."

Stevie interrupted, protesting, "That's not how it goes, Mama."

I asked, "How does it go?"

Stevie replied, "And it came to pass . . ."

Joshua and President Kimball

BARBARA B. SMITH

Before [Joshua] started school his father decided to teach him the Articles of Faith. He wanted to know just how difficult they were for children to memorize for their advancement from the Primary. So each family home night his parents taught him one article of faith. The fourth was hard for him. He didn't have it memorized by bedtime, so his mother said, "Go to bed now, Joshua, and we'll work on the fourth article of faith again tomorrow." Joshua went, but whenever his parents checked on him during the night, there was that little fellow trying to recite the right words. By morning he delightedly exclaimed, "I've got it. I've got it. I can say the fourth article of faith." And he did. He continued on until he had learned nine articles of faith. One day Joshua came with me as I ran an errand to President Spencer W. Kimball's home. I knew Joshua had learned nine articles of faith, so I said, "Joshua, if President

45

Kimball is home perhaps you could say your nine articles of faith for him." He said, "Why? He knows them, doesn't he?" I had to laugh, and as I did President Kimball answered the door. I told him what I was laughing about. He listened and then said, "Well, Joshua, will you say the nine articles of faith for me?"

Joshua did. He didn't make a single mistake, and President Kimball said, "Joshua, when you have learned all thirteen articles of faith, will you come back and say them all to me?" Joshua told his parents about the invitation and worked doubly hard to learn the rest of the Articles of Faith. . . .

. . . It was a happy day when he went to the office and performed for him. President Kimball then said, "Joshua, I am proud of you. Now, when you have memorized the New Testament, come back again."

"Heinous, Heinous, Yay!"

KIMBERLY OTTOSEN

After our stake president reaffirmed the prophet's counsel to read something from the Book of Mormon each day with our families, we decided to follow his counsel, even though our son, Ben, was only one year old. We often felt discouraged with the results. Some nights we were lucky to read one verse; on others, we actually achieved our goal of ten verses. But we persisted. And it came to pass that we reached the book of Enos.

For some reason Ben became overjoyed while we read this selection. That night we actually read Enos straight through—three times! For the next two weeks during our study time, we read Enos again and again. Ben would jump up and down exclaiming, "Heinous (Enos), Heinous, Yay!"

Now Ben is three. He loves scripture time. His current

favorite is Ammon. We don't know why Enos was so important to him, but we do know that by following the prophet's counsel, our family is blessed.

In one Primary's sharing time, the students played a "Who Am I?" game using a figure from each of the standard works. The answer to the "Who Am I?" for the Book of Mormon was the brother of Jared, which the students finally guessed. "But what is his real name?" Without hesitation, one of the boys on the back row called out, "John Jacob Jingleheimer Schmidt!"

—From *Best-Loved Humor of the LDS People*, ed. Linda Ririe Gundry, Jay A. Parry, and Jack M. Lyon, 225.

Holidays

A Children's Play

ANONYMOUS

Stage lights went up at the kindergarten's Christmas pageant, revealing angels, sheep, wise men, and giggling children trying to keep straight faces. This Roman Catholic school's production appeared rather ordinary as far as nativity scenes go. But one aspect of the production was peculiar—there was no written script. The directors had decided that without a script the children would be allowed to speak freely and more naturally. Children know stories better than adults anyway, the saying goes. Very well, said the children. We will do this story as if it were happening to us.

The angels clamored then sang. The shepherds played with the flock. And the children spoke frankly. The parents nodded. Very much how it must have happened, they agreed. Finally, the scene approached where a boy, dressed as an innkeeper, stood in front of a cardboard inn, looking somewhat proud. A girl's clothing was stuffed to make her appear pregnant, and her husband, Joseph, wore a towel around his head, tied with a ribbon. They walked deliberately towards the innkeeper with slow, almost dejected steps. Everything had gone well up to this particular scene.

An austere Joseph approached the inn. The innkeeper answered.

"What do you want?" the stern-faced innkeeper gruffly asked.

"I want a room in the inn."

"We don't have any room."

"But my wife—she's pregnant!" Mary nodded in agreement.

"Well," said the innkeeper with a straight face, "that's not my fault."

The audience roared with delight at the innkeeper's frank reply. The children, not knowing the reason for the laughter but happy enough to be well received, smiled and tried to continue. Joseph decided to join in the conversation.

"Well," his tone rising at the end of the phrase, "it's not my fault either!"

The Truth about the Easter Bunny

BARBARA B. SMITH

It was just before Easter when Melissa announced to her mother, "I know that you [meaning her father and mother] are the Easter bunny, the tooth fairy, and all those guys—except Santa Claus!" She was almost five years old and had been giving those things a lot of thought. She could not believe that a bunny could get down the chimney or hop into each house with its paws filled with Easter baskets, candy eggs, and Easter outfits. It was not plausible to her little mind. Trying to save the excitement of the occasion for her, her father quickly asked, "Do I look like an Easter bunny? Do I have long ears?" He found himself rolling with laughter at her innocent response, "Well, kinda!"

The Anonymous Benefactor

SUSAN EASTON BLACK

I was a graduate student in 1977, completing a doctoral degree and raising three small sons alone. Like several other graduate students, I had obtained university employment as a research writer for a professor; and like most of the students, I was struggling to meet my financial obligations.

Having more "month than money" had become my norm, but never more so than in December 1977. Five days before Christmas, I realized that my mismanagement of funds would prevent any ostentation in gift buying for my children. In fact, it seemed to prevent much gift buying of any kind. It seemed unbearable to me—a young mother who knew all too well how to selfishly flaunt Christmas treasures before less fortunate neighbors, but not how to graciously be one of the less fortunate.

Cuddling my sons, I reluctantly explained my

abhorrence of debt and the specter of our economic plight. My emotions surfaced as the children attempted to comfort me by nodding assuredly, "Don't worry! Santa Claus will give us gifts."

Cautiously I explained, "I think Santa Claus is also having a bad year."

With certainty my firstborn son, Brian, announced, "But on television his sleigh is still filled with toys. With five days left till Christmas, he'll have plenty for us." His younger brother Todd interjected, "Besides, Santa won't forget us. We've been good this year."

As all three nodded in agreement, I did too. My sons had been good. They had found happiness and friendship in our family; we all were unusually close. Perhaps it was our circumstance. Yet, despite their goodness, they would soon be disappointed because neither Santa nor mother would bring the desired presents on Christmas Day.

That night I cried and pled with the Lord for relief, for a glimmer of hope that Christmas in our home would be better than I anticipated. My verbal prayers awakened the children. They seemed to intuitively know what was causing my unhappiness. "Don't worry about presents. It doesn't matter," said Brian. I knew it didn't matter on December 20th, but I knew it would be all-important on December 25th.

The next morning I could not hide the despair and self-pity that had marred my face through the night. "What is wrong?" I was asked again and again at the university. My trite reply was "Nothing." Unconvinced friends pried and seemed in their own way to make matters worse. I snapped at the extended hand of friendship and grimaced at their undue interest in my personal life.

Arriving home, I methodically pulled the mail from the mailbox as I entered the house. A curious, unstamped envelope caught my attention. "To a very, very, very, very, very special lady" was typewritten on the envelope. I gazed at the envelope and wondered if it were meant for me. Hoping it was, I tore it open. To my surprise I found several dollars inside, but not a note of explanation.

"Come quickly," I beckoned my children. Together we counted the money, examined the envelope, and expressed wonder at the anonymous gift. This was a direct answer to my prayer. There was enough money in the envelope to buy an extra gift for each child. I was stunned and amazed, and my joy and excitement of Christmas had returned. It was going to be a great Christmas Day after all. It wouldn't be as lavish as those of my childhood, but it would be good enough.

I was curious. Where had the money come from? Could it be from a neighbor, a friend, a classmate, or the bishop? Logical deduction led me first to near neighbors. Visiting from house to house in our neighborhood proved embarrassing. As I attempted to thank neighbors, each stammered and then confessed, "It wasn't me." Calling friends and thanking them elicited clever expressions. "If you find out who is giving away money, tell them to send some my way." Classmates rendered similar comments.

It must be the bishop, I decided. He knew what I paid in tithing and would be aware that a less than exciting Christmas would be awaiting my family. The children and I walked to his house and knocked on the door. Enthusiastically, we thanked him for his generosity. However, he denied being our benefactor and assured us that he did not know who had been so kind.

Curiosity mounted as nightfall approached. I read the envelope again: "To a very, very, very, very, very special lady." This time I noticed that the "e" and "l" were misshapen letters produced by an old typewriter ribbon. I also observed that each dollar bill had been folded and unfolded many times, as if each one had been of infinite worth. My desire to discover the identity of the anonymous donor grew. Soon that desire was coupled with the gnawing resolve to return the money. The misshapen letters and folded dollar bills evidenced that the generous donor also had financial difficulties.

I couldn't sleep that night. Again and again I asked myself, "Who was it?" I had the clues of the old typewriter ribbon and the folded money, but not the answer. I can't really describe how I finally knew who the benefactor was, but about two o'clock in the morning, I knew. I knew who had a broken typewriter, and who needed to replace their ribbon, and who carefully folded and unfolded money, checking each dollar bill. It was my three sons.

With tears of love, I awoke the donors. Blurry-eyed they asked, "What's wrong?" I replied, "Nothing's wrong; everything is right! You gave me the money. You gave me all the money you possess!" Opening the bedroom closet door, I pulled out three empty jars that once had contained their treasured fortune. They sat silent for several moments until my nine-year-old Brian turned to his younger brother Todd and punched him. "You told!" he exclaimed. Attempting to fend off further blows, Todd yelled, "It wasn't me. It must have been John." Their five-year-old brother immediately said, "It wasn't me," as both boys landed on him. In unison they asked, "How did you know?"

I had searched outside my home for the answer—but the answer was within. I had seen generosity in all those around me, but had failed to recognize the generous hearts of my children. And now I more clearly knew why the Savior had said, "Suffer the little children to come unto me, and forbid them not: for of such is the kingdom of [heaven]" (Mark 10:14; Luke 18:16). My house, with all of its material flaws, was my heaven on earth, and my sons were my greatest treasure. Christmas 1977 was indeed a merry Christmas worth remembering.

Faith in Christ

MIGNON COLEY

One evening while baby-sitting my children, my sister pulled out the New Testament stories for children for their bedtime reading. My daughter was not quite five and had decided that these were her favorite stories because they were about Jesus. She requested to hear the story of the Crucifixion. My sister tried to divert her to a more "child friendly" story that would be easier to understand. She explained to Sarah that Jesus was killed in that story and asked her if she didn't want a happier one that evening.

Sarah responded, "Don't worry, he was resurrected!"

The faith exhibited in Sarah's response has become an example for me and my entire family.

An Easter Egg Hunt

L. E. JACOBSEN

My brother's ward held an Easter activity day with an Easter egg hunt at the home of a ward member who had a very large yard. His ward has a relatively small Primary group, so they were encouraged to invite extended family members and nonmember neighbors to participate. I took my two youngest children to the event.

My five-year-old, only moderately interested in the craft tables set up on one side of the backyard, eventually wandered over to a swing set positioned on the other side of the yard. Consequently he didn't hear the call for his age-group to go to the front yard for the Easter egg hunt. He continued playing on the swings until he noticed one of his cousins coming back with her basket full of candy and eggs. He was quite crestfallen when he realized he'd missed the hunt, and he began to cry. Several other children, without prompting from the adults, offered to share their candy with him, but he was still very upset and continued to cry.

Finally one child ran to the front yard, hid several pieces of her candy, and then came back, telling my son that there was more candy to be found. My son brightened up immediately, and while he was "finding" her candy, many more Primary children ran to the front yard and began hiding pieces of candy. My son had a marvelous time running from one child to the next as the kids called to him to "come look over here!"

What I noticed most about the incident was the sincere generosity of the children. The children didn't hide just the candy they didn't want. The nicer toys and the more desirable chocolate candies were placed in hiding for my son, and the quantities were large. If the adults hadn't told the kids that they had done enough, many would have continued to hide candy until their own baskets were empty. What a wonderful lesson in charity.

"What gift can we give our parents?" the teacher asked her kindergarteners.

"Mud," one boy responded enthusiastically.

"Mud?" the teacher questioned.

"Well, that's what the Wise Men brought Jesus—gold, frankenstein, and mud."

—Brad Wilcox

A Teacher's Christmas

BRAD WILCOX

At holiday time the Christmas spirit is felt by everyone. But I am convinced that there is an extra helping reserved each year just for those who work closely with children. While most people associate Christmas with cards, carols, shopping, and evergreen trees, teachers have additional Yuletide dimensions. For me the season would be incomplete without the smell of paste and construction paper and the glitter that I can't ever get off my hands or out of my hair. December brings thoughts of changing bulletin boards and of tissue-paper "stained glass" windows.

Each year, the "December" file in my filing cabinet gets thicker and thicker as I add new examples of student writing. One girl wrote a story about some robbers holding up a snowman family with blow dryers. A boy wrote an essay entitled "But What If Joseph and Mary Really Wanted a Girl?" Perhaps my favorite is the advice of one sixth grader, who wrote, "Never let your parents think you've stopped believing in Santa Claus or all you'll get is underwear!"

One second grader was explaining the real meaning of Christmas to his teacher: "It's not Frosty," he said, "because everyone knows that snowmen can't talk. It's the real stuff—like Santa Claus."

My mother taught second grade for years. She loves reading a paragraph one of her students wrote: "I am a little present. On Christmas Eve I will be opened. I will be happy because it is hot in here!" Mom also chuckles over the little girl who said, "Susan says there isn't any Santa Claus, and she is in fifth grade! She's old enough to know better than that!"

There is nothing like Christmas in the classroom: one adult surrounded by many children who are too excited to concentrate, too eager to settle down, and too loaded with sugar to stop moving. At times it is so frustrating you consider cutting your whole Christmas list down to just one item: a bottle of aspirin. But then there are the times when a child will hug you on the way out to recess. It's then you truly appreciate the gift it is to share in the indescribable wonder, excitement, and joy that fill children at Christmastime.

A Magical Christmas

RICHARD PETERSON

Our fondest Christmas memories are often those created amid the most modest circumstances.

In November 1947 when I was eight, my father was transferred by his employer from Salt Lake City, where I had been born, to Seattle, Washington. In the booming, post–World War II economy, housing was in short supply all over the United States. Our family of four ended up living for several weeks in a single room in a place called the Sunset Motel—a not-very-fancy facility with eight connected units that faced an asphalt parking lot.

My mother had been reluctant to leave her family, friends, and comfortable home in Salt Lake, and I know now she was homesick and having difficulty adjusting to the typical Northwest rainy weather. With Dad needing our only car to get to work and back, Mom was cooped up day after dreary day in the cramped motel room with my younger sister and me.

As Christmas approached, Dad brought home a small evergreen Christmas tree, which he set up on top of the only dresser in the room. My sister and I had fun decorating it with a few ornaments and a package of the silvery tinsel icicles that were fashionable at that time.

On Christmas Eve, Dad drove us through the rain to a place that had become our favorite place to eat, a drive-in restaurant called Hawk's Hamburgers. We ordered at a drive-up window then took our food back to the motel where we ate while listening to a special Christmas-Eve production of the *Jack Benny Radio Show*.

I don't know how my parents arranged it, but Santa somehow found us that night, and I awoke in the morning to find a brand-new, full-sized J.C. Higgins bicycle at the foot of the bed my sister and I shared. There were other gifts as well, and with Dad home from work, and the four of us together, I remember what might have been a lonely and drab Christmas as one of the most magical of my childhood.

Four-year-old Tanner was sitting on Santa's lap. Santa asked, "Have you been a good boy?"

"Well," Tanner replied honestly, "I've been a little mean."

Santa began to laugh as Tanner continued, "But not as mean as my friend Jacob. Santa, you'll know his house because he has a gray roof."

—Brad Wilcox

Heaven
and
Deity

The Most Important Thing

F. ENZIO BUSCHE

When I was about eleven years old, I gained an understanding of our Heavenly Father's love. My parents were not then very religious but they were good people. They loved me and taught me to be good, clean, and honest, and they helped me to develop righteous desires. Although they were always interested in questions of truth, they did not know God, so they could not tell me about Him. I had an undeveloped hope for the reality of God, but never seemed to find anyone who knew Him and could tell me about Him.

I remember seeing a person killed in an accident. Faced for the first time with death, I was so shaken that I couldn't sleep for a couple of days and became ill. No one could tell me what happens after death. A great fear developed within me that some accident would happen to my father and nobody would be able to explain where he had gone.

Later, during World War II in my home country of Germany, I lived with my mother and four sisters far away from home in southern Germany in two very small, humble rooms. We had fled from our home because of the many air attacks that had destroyed our city and threatened our lives. My father was separated from us because he had been drafted into the army. And I was too young to understand the dramatic events happening around me during that terrible war.

Lying in bed one night in the room I shared with two of my sisters, I remember an intense feeling of loneliness. My mother and two other sisters slept in the next room, but I still felt lost in our temporary home and surroundings. The people even spoke a different dialect than I was used to. I had a most frightening thought: What is the purpose of my being here on this earth? I couldn't answer this question, and it led right into another one that was even more frightening: What is eternity?

I looked into my heart for answers to these questions. But the more I thought about eternity, the more lost I felt. There was nothing to hold onto, nothing to stand on. I had the feeling of falling, falling, falling without stopping. It scared me terribly.

I can still remember the details of that room—the pale light of the moon and the sound of the church clock bell ringing every fifteen minutes. I was awake until early in the morning. And I was so overcome with despair that I began to cry. I wept and wept.

Suddenly something changed. A comforting power enveloped me, and a small voice said to my soul, "You are My child. Have trust in Me."

Immediately joy and happiness filled my heart. All my fear, loneliness, and despair were changed into feelings of warmth and comfort. That night I learned for the first time that there is some unseen but loving Person who is concerned about me. Especially is this true when I feel despair and need help.

A teacher smiled pleasantly at her Primary class. "All right, children, all those who want to go to heaven raise your hands."

Everyone responded but one little boy. "What's the matter, Shawn? Don't you want to go to heaven?" asked the teacher.

"I can't, Sister Nelson. My mom said I had to come straight home."

—From *Best-Loved Humor of the LDS People,* ed. Linda Ririe Gundry, Jay A. Parry, and Jack M. Lyon, 99.

"More Room in Heaven"

LESLIE JENSEN

When our oldest children were three and four years old, we were going somewhere in the car. As we were preparing to back out of the garage, the children began to squabble, as children that age sometimes will.

Their father and I were sitting in the front seat, and wanting to teach them at an early age to be kind to each other, I turned around and said, "If you two can't get along here on earth, how are you going to get along in heaven?" The four-year-old replied, "There's more room in heaven!"

Heavenly Father Knows

AUTHOR UNKNOWN

I teach the six- and seven-year-olds in Primary. One particular Sunday my class was in charge of doing the Primary opening exercises. This included an opening prayer, a scripture, two talks, and finally the closing prayer. All of the children prepared and did an exceptional job on their assigned parts.

When it came time for the closing prayer, the boy I had assigned started the prayer as every child does: "Heavenly Father, thank you for this day. Thank you for our teachers. Please bless . . ." But the little boy couldn't seem to find the right words, so he decided to rephrase his petition. "Please bless those that . . ." Once again, the words weren't coming, so he took yet another approach. "Please bless those that cannot . . . Wait! Please bless those that cannot be better . . . Wait! Please bless those not here, that they'll . . . Wait!"

Suddenly he stopped, paused for a moment, then blurted out, "Oh, you know what I mean!" and closed his prayer.

One night a father called on his five-year-old son, Tommy, to say the blessing on the food. The family closed their eyes and bowed their heads and waited . . . and waited . . . and waited. Finally the father got a little anxious. "Tommy," he prompted. "Go ahead."

"But, Dad," said Tommy, his eyes brimming with tears. "If I thank Heavenly Father for the spinach, won't he know I'm telling a lie?"

—From *Best-Loved Humor of the LDS People*, ed. Linda Ririe Gundry, Jay A. Parry, and Jack M. Lyon, 105–6.

A Young Admirer

PETER B. GARDNER

My three-year-old nephew J.T. receives lots of compliments for tasks well done. When his parents found out he was autistic, they arranged for special tutors to help him learn to communicate and develop basic skills that are especially hard for him. As progress is sometimes slow, they do their best to encourage every little development with cascades of praise such as "You did a great job, J.T." and "Way to go!"

One fall day when J.T. was outside with his mom, she noticed that he was intently observing the yellow leaves of a quaking aspen tree blown by the cool autumn breeze.

"Aren't the trees pretty, J.T.?" she asked. "Jesus made the trees."

After considering this new idea for a moment, J.T replied with much enthusiasm, "Jesus did a great job!"

A Voice of Warning

HAROLD B. LEE

I have a believing heart that started with a simple testimony that came when I was a child—I think maybe I was around ten or eleven years of age. I was with my father out on a farm away from our home, trying to spend the day busying myself until my father was ready to go home. Over the fence from our place were some tumble-down sheds that would attract a curious boy, and I was adventurous. I started to climb through the fence, and I heard a voice as clearly as you are hearing mine, calling me by name and saying, "Don't go over there!" I turned to look at my father to see if he were talking to me, but he was way up at the other end of the field. There was no person in sight. I realized then, as a child, that there were persons beyond my sight, for I had definitely heard a voice. Since then, when I hear or read stories of the Prophet Joseph Smith, I too have known what it means to hear a voice, because I've had the experience.

Which One Was He?

JULIE STEINBERG

Years ago my oldest daughter and I were traveling home after visiting a Primary in the stake. While on the road we got a flat tire. My daughter was about four years old and was absorbed in eating the sack lunch we had packed. I got out of the car and assessed the situation. I had a white dress on, and besides, I didn't know enough about changing a tire to do it myself.

I said to my daughter, "We need to pray to Heavenly Father to help us get our tire changed."

We prayed and then went on eating. Pretty soon a car that had three teenage boys in it pulled off the highway. They quickly changed the tire and refused offers of payment for their services.

"See?" I said to my daughter as I got back in the car, "Heavenly Father did help us."

She looked at the three boys starting to drive away and with the faith of a child said, "Which one was He?"

The Purity of a Child

DEAN WESSENDORF

Years ago when our oldest child was about two, I attended a priesthood meeting that had a strong impact on me. The topic was family home evening. Up to that point my wife and I hadn't held regular family home evenings. We had tried a few times, but we hadn't seen much success. We thought our daughter Jessica was too young to get much out of it, and we weren't that excited about putting on a show for each other. After attending that meeting, however, I was determined to lead my family in regular home evenings.

As I spoke with my wife about it, she agreed that this was important for our family. The very next day, we began holding regular family home evenings. The lesson was on temples. We had a filmstrip, complete with pictures of many temples, including some interior pictures of the Salt Lake Temple. After that short, spirit-filled family home evening, Jessica began sobbing. My wife and I tried in vain to comfort her and to figure out what was bothering her. After about thirty minutes she looked up through her tears and said, "I miss Jesus." Then tears filled our eyes, too, as we thought of the love Jesus and Heavenly Father have for us, the love we have for them, and the purity of a child that brought us to that remembrance.

That moment had a profound impact on me and my wife. As a result, our family of nine has missed only a few family home evenings in more than ten years. What a blessing to be among these special spirits with whom our Father in Heaven has entrusted us! I will always cherish my children and the special moments like this one that bring me back "home," even if only for a brief moment.

The Most Influential People

SHONNA C. DODSON

When my son Joshua was in third grade, I wondered if he was taking his Primary lessons to heart. He was barely learning to write when his elementary school-teacher asked him to write a story about the people who influence his life the most. He came home and started asking me what influence means and how people influence him.

I told him, "People influence you by making you feel better and helping you be a better person." I then told him those people might include his father, myself, or anyone in the family.

A couple of weeks went by, and I did not hear any more on the subject. At the end of the semester I was called into a conference with Joshua's teacher.

She started by saying to me, "Are you religious in some way?"

I told her we were Latter-day Saints and then asked why.

She said, "Well, I want you to see this paper Josh did about people who influence him the most."

I started to read the paper and then began to cry. On the paper was a picture of Jesus and God. Under the picture was this statement: "The people who influence me the most is God. He sent his Son so I could live. He loves everybody and helps us."

To teach a lesson on gratitude for the gifts of fruits and vegetables that our Heavenly Father has provided for our good, I brought examples for the class to eat. While emphasizing that these were "gifts" from our Heavenly Father, an inquisitive and trusting four-year-old asked, "You mean he just stopped by your house last night and gave them to you?"

—Jill Gibson Serfustini

A Child's Testimony

SHANE DIXON

It was fast and testimony meeting. I sat underneath our bench in the North Hollywood Spanish Branch, admiring collected pieces of dried gum that had been stuck to the bottoms of the pews. I suppose, looking back on it all, lying on my back and staring at gum during church service was rather irreverent. But at church my mother handled the workload of controlling three boys all by herself, while my father, who had been called as second counselor in the branch presidency, sat on the stand. Further, it wasn't easy for my brothers and me to listen to the meeting because it was conducted in Spanish, a language my parents knew well but with which my brothers and I were unfamiliar. So sometimes out of boredom, I would slip underneath the pews and look at the multicolored undersides of the benches. This time, however, I grew too disruptive, and my mother motioned for me to sit next to her. Looking back, it certainly is a lucky thing that my mother pulled me into my seat, because what happened next has affected my entire life.

Once seated correctly, I listened with curiosity as a man bore a tearful testimony in Spanish. Even though the words were unfamiliar, I believed I understood what he was saying, and the words touched me. With a resolution that came without warning, I tugged on my mother's dress and told her I wanted to go up to the pulpit. She gave me a serious look (I believe all moms do this), as if she were gauging my sincerity. When she was satisfied I was serious, she led me up to the pulpit.

Once there, standing in front of some two hundred people, I proceeded to "freak out." I began my testimony with a series of strained phrases and long pauses. My testimony, mostly a series of "ums" was hardly coherent, let alone eloquent.

But then again, complete comprehension is seldom achieved in sacrament meeting. Perhaps this is because we are grappling with some of the deepest feelings of our hearts. Even if we don't make sense, most of the time people seem to understand what we are trying to say.

What was it that I wanted to say? I knew that often a testimony lists things the bearer loves. So I stood there wondering what it was that I loved. What had the kids before me said? Maybe I could use one of those lines.

"C'mon," my brain encouraged, "just say you love your Primary teacher and sit down!"

The women in the congregation were shifting uncomfortably in their seats. A bad sign. Men took on an air of understanding, but their eyes betrayed them. I wanted to say something, but I simply couldn't find any words. My eyes watered.

But then a feeling came. Although it was new to me then, it was a feeling on which I would reflect again and again. Even now, more than twenty years later, I often look back and feel the strength of that impression. It was there at that pulpit, speaking English to Spanish speakers, that I first said, "I know that Jesus loves me."

I paused just before I mentioned the Savior. As I attempted to express this impression that had come to me, I became engulfed in emotion, and a knot formed in my throat. I'd never experienced this before, and I was a little scared. But a warm feeling reassured me, and I finished my testimony, although the knot made speaking the words laborious. I knew then, as I said my final words, that the Savior truly did love me.

No angels came down, nor did the heavens open to my view. But the feelings I felt as I bore a new testimony of the Savior were electrifying to me then and remain nourishing to me now. It is remarkable to me that the love of our Savior can be felt by everyone, even by a five-year-old kid who picks at the gum underneath the church seats. I know that the Savior loves me. And I love him for that.

Words of Wisdom

MONTY HAYS

Late one peaceful summer night in 1992, I was helping my not-quite-three-year-old daughter, Elizabeth, into bed. As we were about to say her prayer, someone drove into the parking lot next to the apartment complex in which we lived. The driver of the car proceeded to squeal the car's tires for several seconds, probably burning off an inch of rubber and disturbing everyone in the complex. Peering out the window I muttered, "Jerk," under my breath. I didn't think my daughter could hear me.

A moment later I turned back to her bed, where she was sitting up. Then she asked me, "Daddy, does Jesus love jerks?"

Feeling caught and embarrassed, I answered that, yes, Jesus does indeed love jerks, as well as everyone else. I told her that I was wrong to call that man in the parking lot a jerk and that it wasn't a very Christlike thing for me to say.

"I know, Dad. That's okay," she answered and patted me on the head. Then she added, "Dad, I know more than you."

So she does.

One night my wife and I were tending three of our grandchildren. My wife had become extremely ill, and it had been a stressful night. It was already past the children's bedtime, but they were still up. Finally, I blurted out in somewhat unkind tones to the older two, "Get to bed now!"

They immediately complied, but soon the eldest reappeared with her hands on her hips. "Grandpa, that's not the way Jesus would talk!" she scolded.

Not being in a mood to be corrected by one so young, I retorted, "I'm older than you are so I should know!"

Without a moment's hesitation, she replied, "Well I'm younger than you, and I saw him last!" Bested by a six-year-old!

—N. Roger Anderson Harrah

A Child's Perspective

The Simple Pleasures of Childhood

JANENE WOLSEY BAADSGAARD

If I rub my eyes when I'm in my bed at night," my young son Joseph said, "I see little sparkly lights floating around in the air."

"Are they all different colors?" I asked.

"Yeah," he answered.

"I used to see them too when I was a little girl," I said. "I thought I was the only one who knew they were there. I don't see those lights anymore. When I'm in my bed now, I just go to sleep."

"Why, Mom? Why don't you like those little lights anymore?"

"It's not that I don't like them," I answered. "I've just forgotten about them," and, I thought, a lot of other important things:

Cheese-its
dragonfly wings
eating peanut butter from a tablespoon
giggling
hopscotch
where the best bird nests are
tree houses
rolling down grassy hills after sundown
pennies
meadowlarks at dawn
stars
bumblebees in clover
squirt guns
dancing in a new petticoat
hollyhocks
climbing trees
dandelions
studying the ceiling, wondering what it would be
    like to live upside down
bubble gum
eating dessert first
snake-grass
making a mess without worrying about how to get
    the stains out
green apples
eating chocolate without worrying about the
    bathroom scales
rope swings

"When you tuck me in tonight," Joseph said, "I'll show you the little sparkly lights again if you want me to."

I have a feeling Joseph will continue to show me the light for many years to come.

Dark eyes aflame with the wonder of discovery, our bubbly five-year-old granddaughter, Rebecca, met me at the door. "Grandma," she began, "you know what?"

"What?" my dutiful reply came.

"When I grow up and get old like mother, she will be really old, old, old, just like you!"

—Irene Fuja

Our oldest child, then about two or three, heard us say many times that he'd been sent to keep us on the straight and narrow path. He added, "Not the wide and wiggly."

—Rebecca Chambers

The Good Food

NONA L. BRADY

I don't remember why Dougie came into the kitchen that day. I just remember seeing his tummy showing below the bottom of a too-small shirt. I was a young mother with a student husband and four children under the age of seven. Money was always tight, and seeing that little tummy—which meant he was growing out of his clothes—was nearly more than I could take.

I looked down at him and half-jokingly and half-accusingly asked, "Dougie, have you been growing again?"

He hung his little blond head and solemnly answered, "Ye-es."

In mock exasperation, I threw my hands in the air and asked, "Why?"

His response was immediate. He raised his head, and with a huge smile he said, "From the good food!"

My financial worries didn't seem nearly so large as I hugged that sweet little boy and sent him out to play.

The rewards of mothering are not immediate. There are times when you are less than appreciated. I took from the oven one day what I thought was a beautiful casserole, only to have my six-year-old son say, "Mom, how come you baked the garbage?"

—Marjorie Pay Hinckley
From *Glimpses into the Life and Heart of Marjorie Pay Hinckley,* ed. Virginia H. Pearce, 61.

Six-year-old Whitney had a string of bad luck and ended up hurting her chin several times in the same week. When she scraped it yet again, she cried, "If my chin gets hurt again, I think it's going to say, 'I quit being on this face!'"

—Brad Wilcox

"Poor, Yet Possessing All Things"

JOYCE BAGGERLY

The first time I saw Jocyln, I thought she was four years old. She was seven. Her bony arms and legs stuck out from a dress that I would have cut up for rags. Her black hair was badly cut in a fringe of bangs across her forehead and looked as if it had never seen a hairbrush in the back—it stuck out in divergent angles. My first thought was that she looked like the starving children featured in humanitarian aid advertisements in women's magazines. She didn't have the extended stomach of a malnourished child, but she looked so frail that I flinched when I took her tiny hand in mine to shake hands.

Shaking hands with the sister missionaries was a ritual for all Filipino children, even if the children weren't Church members. Any visitor to the squatters' huts was instantly surrounded by children. They chirped away in Tagalog, which my Filipina companion understood, of

94

course. I had only a smile and a handshake as means of communication. Jocyln looked more timid than most of the children, standing back from the crowd until her mother called and insisted that she shake my hand. A new American missionary, especially an older one, was an event not to be missed.

When we were formally introduced, I learned that her name was Jocyln. I explained to her, with my Filipina companion acting as translator, that my first name was the same as hers, just a different version of it. Perhaps that is why she seemed to love to be near me. Whenever I saw her at Church or when we were visiting her family, Joclyn would shyly stand next to me, waiting patiently to see if I would put my arm around her. When I did, she would lean her head on my shoulder. The first time that happened, I was startled to discover that the back of her head was completely flat. Our mission president, a medical doctor, said that as a newborn she'd probably been put on her back for extremely long periods of time, so her skull was formed by whatever hard surface she'd been put on. We asked him if there was anything that could be done. He said he'd examine her, but he thought there was probably nothing that could be done at her age. Worries about her health added to the growing despair I felt as I continued to get sicker.

Upon arriving in the Philippines, I had quickly realized that I would have a very difficult time because of my many allergies. The longer I was there, the more hives I had and the more hoarse my voice became. I was holding on by sheer willpower and was determined to stay.

That determination came from my deep love of the people. Jocyln's family, for example, had been baptized, and the ward members were fellowshipping them, but since they were fairly new converts, we missionaries could continue to visit them and teach them basic gospel principles. We loved them so dearly and took every opportunity to be with them. As soon as they had heard the gospel, every member of the family had accepted with true love and devotion. They immediately started attending Church and paying tithing on their very meager earnings. Once when we needed a dress for an investigator to be able to come to church, the mother of this family gave us one of her two dresses—the better one, of course.

When the decision was made to transfer me back to the United States, a black cloud such as I had never felt before settled over me. At the age of forty-eight, I'd had plenty of life's disappointments to deal with, but now I felt as if I were deserting a people who desperately needed what I could give them. I realize now that I was so sick that I had become all wrapped in "me" and not what the Lord wanted, which is why the cloud of despair hung over me. Jocyln would be the key to lifting that cloud.

The last Sunday I labored in the Philippines, my companion and I walked Jocyln's family home from a fireside. The quickest way to their hut was along the railroad tracks that ran down the middle of the squatters' huts. As sad as I was at leaving the country, I was even sadder at leaving this wonderful, humble family, probably never to see them again in mortality. As we walked down the railroad tracks toward her hut, she took my hand and began to jump from railroad tie to tie. She was so tiny, so frail that I was reluctant to propel her as I would have a healthy American child. Jocyln had other ideas. I glanced back at her mother to make sure that it was all right, and receiving a nod and a grin, we set off laughing and squealing as I launched her as high and as far as she wanted. Jocyln knew she had the strength; I was the doubter. She knew her tiny, thin arms were strong enough to take the swing and her scrawny legs could endure the landing. Jocyln knew she would land on her feet, ready to spring forward to the next tie. I was the one who thought she needed protection.

Jocyln, poor by the world's standards, showed me, who is rich beyond all understanding by Filipino standards, that she and her people were fine because the gospel was being taught and accepted. Her family possessed all things necessary to make them rich by celestial standards—they had each other, and now they had the gospel.

As we went that quarter of a mile, jumping and laughing like a couple of happy children, a verse from a favorite scriptural passage came into my mind with the enlightenment that comes only from the Holy Ghost. It described Jocyln and the people of the Philippines: "As sorrowful, yet alway rejoicing; as poor, yet making many rich; as having nothing, and yet possessing all things" (2 Corinthians 6:10).

If I were in charge of the world, I'd cancel war, bullies, and weirdos. I would have more friends, peace, books, and airplanes would all be safe. If I were in charge of the world, every person would eat his meals, drugs would all be burned, and people would never be lonely.

—Miranda Wilcox, age nine

Reverently, Quietly
SUSAN A. SANDBERG

My grown son's name has brought him a bit of extra attention from time to time. Lehi now loves his name and proudly goes by it, but that was not so in the past.

Lehi noticed at a very early age that his name was often mentioned in meetings. His worried conviction that "everyone was talking about him" led us to nickname him Lee.

When Lehi was five years old and I was a teacher in his Primary, he passed by me on the way to class, arms folded, with an intense about-to-cry expression on his face. Since he was a very serene child, this concerned me, and I stopped him and took him in my arms.

"What is it, son?" I asked. His poor little face collapsed in anguish as he told me his woes: "Mommy, why don't they talk about anyone else? I'm a good boy! I don't be bad!" As I wondered what could have happened, he went on to explain that the children had just sung a familiar Primary song.

"Mommy, they said, 'Reverent, Lee! Quiet, Lee! Soft, Lee! Now we sing to thee. . . .'" His voice then dissolved into pitiful sobs, feeling very persecuted. Unable to suppress my laughter, I comforted my broken-hearted child. When we returned home, I took on the daunting task of trying to explain adverbs to a five-year-old.

My nearly thirty-year-old son still cringes when this treasured family story is told.

One Sunday as I was leading the junior Primary singing time, I was reviewing with the children a simple prayer song we had been learning. I reminded the children that the phrases rhymed and then proceeded to repeat the first line and pause for them to complete the second. "Thanks to our Father we will bring, For he gives us . . ." One bright three-year-old piped up in perfect rhythm "Bur-ger King!"

—Eva Garlick

"What Makes You Have a Bad Day?"

MARSHA ROSE STEED

Father in Heaven gave me a gift of sunshine in a freckle-faced package. Since the time he was tiny, Kevin has been the proverbial "seeker of wisdom." At age three, he wanted to know what blood was made of. I explained, ever the patient mother that I am, that blood was composed of red and white blood cells and corpuscles. He had to know what each thing looked like and asked me to show him a picture! Exasperated, I finally asked him why he wanted to know. He replied, "Mom, I have to know things." Thus it went for the next few years. He taught me more than I've ever taught him. Fistfuls of dandelions reminded me to pause and see what was around me.

Yet the greatest insight, for which I will thank him all the days of my life, came when he was in kindergarten.

Kevin's teacher and I were having a parent-teacher conference. With him, these have always been a joy. His teacher proceeded to relate to me just what sort of child I had in my home. She said that one day she was patiently telling the class about "bad days" and how it was all right if sometimes they felt sad or didn't get along. Sometimes she said she had bad days when the students wouldn't put their names on their papers or they didn't want to listen. To get her point across, she asked the class for examples.

"Kevin, what makes you have a bad day?"

Kevin, she said, thought and thought, then shrugged his shoulders and replied, "I don't know. . . . I've never had one."

I'm grateful for this little ball of sunshine that the Lord has given us. Things are often far from perfect, but Kevin always reminds me that each day is to be cherished as the good gift it is.

Blessings for Eva

PETER B. GARDNER

My brother tells the story of finding a "golden family" while serving his mission in London, England. The family, which had recently emigrated from East Africa, was still struggling to learn English. So the missionaries kept their words simple and used lots of gestures to communicate. To involve the young children, the elders sang Primary songs and played games with them. They quickly found their way into the hearts of each member of the family—except for one. Four-year-old Eva was determined not to be so easily won over as her adoring brother and sisters had been by these white-skinned strangers.

But one day the elders witnessed "a mighty change of heart" in this little soul. After the missionaries sang "Choose the Right," Eva's eyes opened wide, and an uncharacteristic smile found its way onto her face. She asked them to sing it again, and this time when they finished she clapped her hands with glee, pleading with the missionaries for yet another encore performance.

Pleased but bewildered to find themselves so suddenly in Eva's good graces, the missionaries asked her why that song made her so happy. In explanation she repeated the final line of the song as she understood it: "Choose the right, and God will bless you, Eva, more!"

Mom was helping two-year-old Henry with his prayers one night. She would say a line, then have him repeat it. The prayer was going well until Mom said, "I thank thee for all thy blessings."

Henry responded graciously, "You're welcome."

—From *Best-Loved Humor of the LDS People,* ed. Linda Ririe Gundry, Jay A. Parry, and Jack M. Lyon, 98.

"My Body *Is* the Happy"

LINDA J. AND RICHARD EYRE

Here is a conversation I had with my three-year-old.

"Why do you have a body?"

"To skip with!"

"To skip with?"

"Yes."

"I see. What's the best part of your body?"

"The eyes."

"Why?"

"'Cause I see the flowers."

"Oh?"

"But the nose is too, 'cause I smell them."

"Do you hear them?"

"No, but if you close your eyes you do hear teensy little things."

"Like what?"

"Wind and trees."

"How do they sound?"

"Swish, swish, but quieter than that."

"Any other parts of the body you like?"

"The tongue to talk—you hold onto it and you can't talk—try it—say my name."

"Unghun—uwam."

"See!" (Laughter)

"Shawni, does your body make you happy?"

"My body *is* the happy!"

Two-year-old David was showing off his knowledge of colors by telling me the colors he saw in my eyes: brown, black, and vanilla.

—Brad Wilcox

Trying to help my two-year-old daughter focus on the sacrament, I helped her take a piece of bread and then whispered, "What will the deacons bring next, Natalie?" Her eyes lit up as she shouted hopefully, "Strawberries?"

—Emily Watts

Authority to Baptize

M. KATHERINE EDWARDS

Back in 1960 my oldest daughter, Jennifer, was riding in a car with her father, who was the branch president of our small branch in Ohio. Realizing that Jennifer would be eight years old that year, her father turned the conversation to the special event that would soon occur in her life. He asked her several questions, testing her knowledge of the subject of baptism. He asked her, "Who has the authority to baptize you, Jennifer?"

Her answer came quickly, "An elder or a priest." Her father continued questioning, "What if he is a high priest?"

She answered seriously, "It doesn't matter how tall he is, as long as he is a priest or an elder."

Trying to maintain the seriousness of the interview, he asked the next question, "What if he's a seventy?"

Little Jennifer answered, "Dad, it really doesn't

matter how old he is, just as long as he is a priest or an elder."

My husband interviewed many members throughout his long years as branch president and bishop, but his memory of this interview with his young daughter always brings him a smile.

One evening a member of the bishopric called and said he'd like to stop by on his way home to talk to my husband. When he arrived, my three-year-old daughter answered the door. Staring at him intently, she followed him to the couch, climbed up beside him, looked him right in the face, and said, "Why are you wearing clothes?" Lucky for us he's got a quick sense of humor and realized that she meant "Why aren't you wearing a suit?"

—Lisa Selby

Spilt Milk

CHAR GWYN

When my daughter Jeannie was about five years old, she liked to try new things. One morning she attempted to pour herself a glass of milk from a nearly full gallon jug. I was standing nearby and knew that there was going to be a bit of a mess, but I wanted her to try anyway.

Well, sure enough, milk splashed out and onto the table. Wanting to be patient and encouraging, I said, "That's okay, honey. The important thing is that no milk got on the carpet!"

Her answer, as she peered over the edge of her glass, was "No, the important thing is I got some in the glass."

The Grand Amen

VALERIE BUCK

When the morning of my baptism arrived, I was worried because my family had moved to a new city one month before, and I didn't know anyone. At the stake center a lady named Sister Adams met us outside the room where eight-year-olds and their families were gathering. Inside I saw a flash of white and stared. There stood a blond, pink-faced boy wearing a white jumpsuit that showed his shins. The boy looked like a white-washed version of the picture on my book *The Adventures of Tom Sawyer,* a boy sprouting out of backwoods clothes in which he grew too fast to fit. I was glad I was a girl and didn't have to wear a jumpsuit.

A week earlier I had cornered Mom for a serious discussion about white clothing. I didn't have a white dress. "The stake provides it," Mom said. "So you'll wear a Sunday dress to the stake center and change into white clothes there."

This eased my worries. A nice white dress was something I had dreamed would help make my baptism as important as it should be.

I was worried that my baptism wouldn't mean much because no one in the audience knew me. In our old ward I had watched my older brother Steve's baptism go perfectly—no foot or clothes coming up. He came up gasping and spluttering, and the audience of people I had known all my life responded in a warm chuckle. They were delighted and approving, and this made the event memorable somehow. I wanted the same thing for me.

Sister Adams led us to the dressing room behind the font. The air was warm and heavy, like the air around an indoor swimming pool. A door in the opposite wall stood off the floor so that beneath it I could see reflected light wavering on the tile like rippling water. I stood watching it, trying to figure out how water could reflect light onto the floor, when our escort lifted up and shook out a white jumpsuit.

I stared in dismay. The moment the lady disappeared, I whirled on Mom.

"Mom, this is for a boy. Don't they have any dresses?"

"No. This is what everyone's starting to use because dresses float up."

"But—"

"Come on. Sister Adams is going to bring someone else in here in a minute. Don't worry. Everyone will be wearing the same thing."

With Mom hurrying me, I scrambled into the jump-suit. I took one look in a wall mirror and saw . . . a whitewashed Tom Sawyer with a ponytail.

I didn't want to go into the room where everyone waited. But, face hot, I padded on white-stockinged feet behind Mom into the room, which was rapidly filling with people.

A line of eight-year-olds in jumpsuits sat on the front row, swinging their legs and ogling the water in the font. I eyed the water too, some of my excitement returning. A mirror angled over the font so that everyone in the audience would have a view of the baptisms. I sat down and looked at my compatriots.

There, on the very last chair, sat a girl in a gleaming white dress, lacy white stockings, and with a white ribbon braided elaborately into her hair.

I stared in indignation. If there had been a chance that anyone in the room besides my family would notice my baptism, it was gone now.

Suddenly an idea came to me: the gasping and sputtering that my brother had done. That had made everyone smile. As I sat through the beginning speeches of the service, I pretended reverence but thought only of how my baptism would work. I had been shown how to stand, where to put my arms, and how to hold my nose. I would do all that, and then when I came up from the water, I would gasp and spit and splutter.

Sister Adams finally announced that we would proceed alphabetically. She read the names, and mine was third. The first boy walked down into the water with his father. I watched the baptismal stance, the prayer, the immersion, and my excitement returned with a flutter. After one more, it would be me.

But the girl in the dress was next.

She walked prettily in her lacy stockings down into the water, in no danger of her dress floating up. Her ribbon gleamed in the mirror. I would be next, and the back half of the room might not even know I was a girl! I stared at her dress, but then I saw her face. Her forehead was wrinkled, her eyes worried. She was frightened. As her father helped her arrange her arms, she trembled. I remembered suddenly all the other things that come with baptism: the being good and kind and loving.

I couldn't help the girl now, but I wished I could have given her the tips that I had received. When the baptismal prayer ended, she clenched her eyes and lips shut in panic and went stiffly under the water. I felt sorry for her.

Remembering what baptism was about, I felt excited again. I was next. I was self-conscious of my jumpsuit as I walked from the front row, but I had eyes only for the water. Dad went down one set of steps, met me at the top of the other, and led me into the water. We stood in the baptismal stance, my heart pounding as I readied to plug my nose. Dad said the prayer, brought down his arm, and firmly lowered me into the water.

Up I came, heavy with water, feeling it rush off me, breathing quickly in completely unfeigned reaction. Dad was leading me up into Mom's waiting towel before I realized I had forgotten to give my gasp and splutter. I turned quickly and looked at Dad. He smiled at me with bright eyes, then looked at Mom, where his smile deepened. I glanced at Mom and saw a mirroring smile—deep, proud, and content. Her smile didn't change when she turned it on me.

On the drive home I considered my failure to draw chuckles from the audience. I lifted my wet hair to tickle my lips and remembered my parents' smiles. I saw that my baptism was like a prayer. For my brother's "prayer," the audience's reaction had been a kind of amen. But my amen was the smiles on my parents' faces and my understanding of what those smiles meant. I didn't need an audience to tell me I had done something important. The warm amen I felt in my heart was enough.

We were playing restaurant for family night, and Wendee was the server. She came to take my order, and I said, "I'll have a hamburger."

She got upset and said, "Dad, this is a Chinese restaurant. You have to order lasagna or spaghetti."

—Brad Wilcox

114

Faith, Courage, and Determination

"I Will Have My Father . . . Hold Me in His Arms"

LUCY MACK SMITH

The surgeon was called again, and he this time enlarged the wound, cutting the leg even to the bone. It commenced healing the second time, and as soon as it began to heal it also began to swell again, which swelling continued to rise till we deemed it wisdom to call a council of surgeons; and when they met in consultation they decided that amputation was the only remedy.

Soon after coming to this conclusion, they rode up to the door and were invited into a room apart from the one in which Joseph lay. They being seated, I addressed them thus: "Gentlemen, what can you do to save my boy's leg?" They answered, "We can do nothing; we have cut it open to the bone and find it so affected that we consider his leg incurable and that amputation is absolutely necessary in order to save his life."

117

This was like a thunderbolt to me. I appealed to the principal surgeon, saying, "Dr. Stone, can you not make another trial? Can you not, by cutting around the bone, take out the diseased part, and perhaps that which is sound will heal over, and by this means you will save his leg? You will not, you must not, take off his leg, until you try once more. I will not consent to let you enter his room until you make me this promise."

After consulting a short time with each other, they agreed to do as I had requested, then went to see my suffering son. One of the doctors, on approaching his bed, said, "My poor boy, we have come again." "Yes," said Joseph, "I see you have; but you have not come to take off my leg, have you, sir?" "No," replied the surgeon, "it is your mother's request that we make one more effort, and that is what we have now come for."

The principal surgeon, after a moment's conversation, ordered cords to be brought to bind Joseph fast to a bedstead; but to this Joseph objected. The doctor, however, insisted that he must be confined, upon which Joseph said very decidedly, "No, doctor, I will not be bound, for I can bear the operation much better if I have my liberty."

"Then," said Dr. Stone, "will you drink some brandy?"

"No," said Joseph, "not one drop."

"Will you take some wine?" rejoined the doctor. "You must take something, or you can never endure the severe operation to which you must be subjected."

"No," exclaimed Joseph, "I will not touch one particle of liquor, neither will I be tied down; but I will tell you what I will do—I will have my father sit on the bed and hold me in his arms, and then I will do whatever is necessary in order to have the bone taken out." Looking at me, he said, "Mother, I want you to leave the room, for I know you cannot bear to see me suffer so; father can stand it, but you have carried me so much, and watched over me so long, you are almost worn out." Then looking up into my face, his eyes swimming in tears, he continued. "Now, mother, promise me that you will not stay, will you? The Lord will help me, and I shall get through with it."

To this request I consented, and getting a number of folded sheets, and laying them under his leg, I retired, going several hundred yards from the house in order to be out of hearing.

The surgeons commenced operating by boring into the bone of his leg, first on one side of the bone where it was affected, then on the other side, after which they broke it off with a pair of forceps or pincers. They thus took away large pieces of the bone. When they broke off the first piece, Joseph screamed out so loudly, that I could not forbear running to him. On my entering the room, he cried out, "Oh, mother, go back, go back; I do not want you to come in—I will try to tough it out, if you will go away."

When the third piece was taken away, I burst into the room again—and oh, my God! what a spectacle for the mother's eye! The wound torn open, the blood still gushing from it, and the bed literally covered with blood. Joseph was pale as a corpse, and large drops of sweat were rolling down his face, whilst upon every feature was depicted the utmost agony!

I was immediately forced from the room, and detained until the operation was completed; but when the act was accomplished, Joseph put upon a clean bed, the room cleared of every appearance of blood, and the instruments which were used in the operation removed, I was permitted again to enter.

Joseph immediately commenced getting better, and from this onward, continued to mend until he became strong and healthy. When he had so far recovered as to be able to travel, he went with his uncle, Jesse Smith, to Salem, for the benefit of his health, hoping the sea-breezes would be of service to him, and in this he was not disappointed.

Having passed through about a year of sickness and distress, health again returned to our family, and we most assuredly realized the blessing; and indeed, we felt to acknowledge the hand of God, more in preserving our lives through such a tremendous scene of affliction, than if we had, during this time, seen nothing but health and prosperity.

Ballad of the Tempest

JAMES THOMAS FIELDS

We were crowded in the cabin,
Not a soul would dare to sleep,—
It was midnight on the waters,
And a storm was on the deep.

'Tis a fearful thing in winter
To be shattered by the blast,
And to hear the rattling trumpet
Thunder, "Cut away the mast!"

So we shuddered there in silence,—
For the stoutest held his breath,
While the hungry sea was roaring
And the breakers talked with death.

As thus we sat in darkness,
Each one busy with his prayers,

"We are lost!" the captain shouted,
As he staggered down the stairs.

But his little daughter whispered,
As she took his icy hand,
"Isn't God upon the ocean,
Just the same as on the land?"

Then we kissed the little maiden,
And we spake in better cheer,
And we anchored safe in harbor
When the morn was shining clear.

My children and I were in the car, going to visit a sister in the ward. On the way, my four-year-old daughter was telling me what she had learned in Primary about faith. She said, "Faith is like a seed."

My other daughter, who was twenty-one months old, remembered that we had just filled the bird feeder with seeds and said, "Birdie ate the faith."

—Kevin and Cathy Kennington

Bricks or Straw?

ARDETH GREENE KAPP

I have a little six-year-old niece, Shelly, who proudly and frequently reminds me that she is made of bricks.

This summer while she was taking a hike with her mother and father, what was intended to be a three-mile hike turned out to be a fourteen-mile hike, due to the misinterpretation of a sign and the loss of direction. After several miles, these unseasoned hikers came to a gradual halt at the crest of a little hill. While sitting down for a welcome rest, Shelly's mother determined to make the best of the situation and use it as a teaching opportunity. She explained to Shelly that this would be a chance to see if they were made of bricks or straw. The comparison had a familiar ring because of the favorite childhood story "The Three Little Pigs." She explained that their final destination was still the camp, so that while the change of plans from three miles to fourteen

miles was somewhat discouraging, it was not distress-
ing, because they were not lost; they knew where they
were going.

This sounded like an adventuresome opportunity to
Shelly, and not realizing the full impact of the situation,
she was anxious to end their brief rest in order to "find
out what we are made of."

Like many teaching and growing opportunities, the
newness and novelty soon wore off and then the real
lesson and testing began. Driven by the desire to "find
out what we are made of," this little six-year-old kept
walking and walking. Though she welcomed the little
rest periods that became more frequent as the day wore
on, something within her nature would not let her give
up. Sometimes she would hold her dad's hand, which
was always close, and sometimes her mother's; but
never did she suggest being carried or giving up.

Near the end of the day, just as the sun was setting,
Shelly's face was flushed and sunburned, smudged from
the frequent brush of her dusty hands across her face to
get the hair out of her eyes. Her sneakers were coated
with dust that had crept up past her socks and blended
into the suntan on her short, tired legs. Without any
complaint, and not being aware of the location of the
camp, she finally stopped, exhausted, to make an
accounting. Shoulders drooping and hands hanging
limply at her side, she said, "Mom, I guess I'm made of
straw."

At this moment her mother let go of her hand,

dropped down on one knee, wrapped the little girl in her arms, and explained, "No, my dear, you are made of bricks. Our camp is in sight, and we have made it, the full fourteen miles."

Together the parents picked up this little soul who had gone as far as she could and only then had stopped to make an accounting. Their rejoicing was beyond measure as they passed the finish line into camp. Now on frequent occasions Shelly reports, with renewed confidence, "I can do it 'cause I'm made of bricks."

When we too have gone as far as we can, we can be sure the camp will be in sight, and we will feel the security of the Lord's arms enfolding us if we don't give up when the going gets tough—and it will.

"What If You Die, Mom?"

DANIEL QUILLEN

Several years ago my wife contracted cancer. One of the steps in the process of dealing with the cancer was informing our children of the diagnosis and the changes that we could expect in our lives as we fought the disease. We gathered our five children together and shared the news. The children had lots of questions, and we answered them to the best of our abilities.

That evening my wife was putting our eight-year-old son, J.D., to bed. With a child's innocence and a quiver in his voice, J.D. asked, "Mom, if you die, who will help Dad take care of us?"

My wife was somewhat taken back by the abruptness of the question. She answered as best as she could: "J.D., it's way too soon to be thinking about things like that. We don't think that will be necessary. We just have to have faith that everything will work out all right."

J.D. replied, "Yes, but what if you do die? Who would help Dad take care of us?"

Again, she replied, "Well, we haven't really thought about it, but I suppose Grandma would come and help Daddy take care of you. But," she added again, "we just have to have faith that everything will be fine." That seemed to calm his troubled mind, and he went to sleep quickly.

J.D. is our deep thinker and often comes up with questions that belie his age. The next evening as my wife tucked him into bed, J.D. said, "Mom, do you remember last night that you said that we had to have faith that everything would be all right?" My wife responded that she remembered having said that. J.D. continued, "But Mom, people with faith die, too."

This insightful comment gave my wife the opportunity to teach our young son about the plan of salvation and help him understand this difficult experience in our lives.

These events occurred seven years ago. Since her surgery and subsequent chemotherapy, my wife has been cancer-free.

"Throw It Here, Sissy!"

HEBER J. GRANT

Because I was] an only child, my mother reared me very carefully. Indeed, I grew more or less on the principle of a hothouse house plant, the growth of which is "long and lanky" but not substantial. I learned to sweep, and to wash and wipe dishes, but did little stone throwing and little indulging in those sports which are interesting and attractive to boys, and which develop their physical frames. Therefore, when I joined a baseball club, the boys of my own age and a little older played in the first nine; those younger than I played in the second, and those still younger in the third, and I played with them.

One of the reasons for this was that I could not throw the ball from one base to the other. Another reason was that I lacked physical strength to run or bat well. When I picked up a ball, the boys would generally shout:

"Throw it here, sissy!"

So much fun was engendered on my account by my youthful companions that I solemnly vowed that I would play baseball in the nine that would win the championship of the Territory of Utah.

My mother was keeping boarders at the time for a living, and I shined their boots until I saved a dollar which I invested in a baseball. I spent hours and hours throwing the ball at Bishop Edwin D. Woolley's barn, which caused him to refer to me as the laziest boy in the Thirteenth Ward. Often my arm would ache so that I could scarcely go to sleep at night. But I kept on practicing and finally succeeded in getting into the second nine of our club. Subsequently I joined a better club, and eventually played in the nine that won the championship of the territory and beat the nine that had won the championship for California, Colorado, and Wyoming. Having thus made good my promise to myself, I retired from the baseball arena.

"He Blessed Me That
I Might Be Healed"

GEORGE ALBERT SMITH

When I was a child I became very ill. The doctor said I had typhoid fever and should be in bed for at least three weeks. He told mother to give me no solid food, but to have me drink some coffee.

When he went away, I told mother that I didn't want any coffee. I had been taught that the Word of Wisdom, given by the Lord to Joseph Smith, advised us not to use coffee.

Mother had brought three children into the world and two had died. She was unusually anxious about me.

I asked her to send for Brother Hawks, one of our ward teachers. He was a worker at the foundry and a poor and humble man of great faith in the power of the Lord.

He came, administered to me, and blessed me that I might be healed.

When the doctor came the next morning I was playing outside with the other children. He was surprised. He examined me and discovered that my fever was gone, and that I seemed to be well.

I was grateful to the Lord for my recovery. I was sure that He had healed me.

Our daughter was intrigued by a quail's nest in our backyard and prayed for the eggs often. One day we noticed that the eggs had all hatched and the quail were gone. Our daughter was disappointed about not getting to see the baby quail and prayed she'd somehow get to see them. Several days later when she was sitting by the window, she exclaimed, "The quail! The quail!" Two adult quail and the same number of chicks as there had been eggs walked through our backyard. In just a minute they were gone, but she had seen them and knew they had come in answer to her sweet prayer.

—Rebecca Chambers

Fasting for Grandma

WILMA AEBISCHER

In 1997 I suffered a nearly fatal heart attack. Upon receiving a phone call from his father, my youngest son and his wife decided that he should leave as soon as he could get a flight out of California. John, who was nine years old at the time, said to his parents, "I am going to fast for Grandma."

"Me too," piped in his seven-year-old sister, Heather.

They were told that they could fast one meal, which seemed to please them. Later when they broke their fast, John gave a beautiful prayer, asking Heavenly Father to please make Grandma well. I received a letter written in his hand while I was in the hospital.

It read, "Dear Grandma, Heavenly Father is going to make you all well, so you can be here when I go on my mission." The faith of these children was indeed answered by the Lord. I survived that serious heart attack, plus two others that year, and I am looking forward to attending John's missionary farewell in seven more years.

My young grandson Paul . . . could hardly wait for his entrance into kindergarten, but he was not thrilled when told about the physical and dental examinations that must precede it. He sat waiting in the dentist's office, and one could see his mounting tension. When the nurse said, "Paul, the doctor is ready for you now," his little body trembled nervously. His mother asked, "Do you want me to go with you?" It was a very serious little man who said, "No thank you, Mother. If I am big enough to go to school alone, I should be big enough to sit in the dentist's chair alone."

–Barbara B. Smith
From *Growth in Grandmothering,* 107.

Saving the Book of Commandments

MARY ELIZABETH ROLLINS LIGHTNER

When the mob [at Independence, Missouri, in 1833] was tearing down the printing office, a two story building [in which the Book of Commandments was being printed], driving Brother [William W.] Phelps' family out of the lower part of the house, they (the mob) brought out some large sheets of paper, saying, "Here are the Mormon commandments." My sister [Caroline], 12 years old (I was then 14) and myself were in a corner of a fence watching them. When they spoke about them being the commandments, I was determined to have some of them. So while their backs were turned, prying out the gable end of the house, we ran and gathered up all we could carry in our arms. As we turned away, two of the mob got down off the house and called for us to stop, but we ran as fast as we could, through a gap in the fence into a large corn field, and the two men after us. We ran a long way in the field, laid the papers on the ground, then laid down on top of them. The corn was very high and thick. They hunted all around us, but did not see us. After we were satisfied they had given up the search, we tried to find our way out of the field. The corn was so tall we thought we were lost. On looking up we saw some trees that had been girdled to kill them. We followed them and came to an old log stable, which looked like it had not been used for years. Sister Phelps and family were there, carrying in brush and piling it up on one side of the stable to make their beds on. She asked us what we had. We told her and also how we came by them. She took them and placed them between her beds. Subsequently Oliver Cowdery bound them in small books and gave me one.

Gospel Principles

The Building Fund Goat

ELDON ROSS PALMER

The year was 1981 when the branch president called me into his office. I stepped in with the fear of eternal damnation twisting my gut; I knew it was time for retribution for my disruptions in Primary. However, President Dosher flashed his disarming white smile and a reassuring chuckle escaped his lips as he saw the panic evident in my wide eyes. My fear soon changed to awe, when, instead of reprimanding me, he handed me a shiny silver dollar. "This is the Lord's money," he cautioned, "given to you to invest in a money-making project for the building fund." He then continued to explain how the branch was growing out of the one-room schoolhouse that served as our church building and how it was the members' responsibility to supply a significant portion of the needed funds for a new building.

Although I didn't pay much attention to the affairs of the branch at my young age, this explanation about the building fund wasn't new to me. My previously carefree life was currently wracked with the exquisite torment of child labor in a raspberry patch and potato field planted by branch members to earn money for the new building. Under the watchful eyes of my parents, I grudgingly helped weed rows, pick berries, and dig potatoes, all as my precious youth wasted away. But the idea of my own project somehow captured my interest. I left the president's office with the pride of responsibility swelling my chest. After all, I had been given a whole dollar!

With the deep, cunning wisdom of an eight-year-old, I schemed and planned for a magnificent project in which I could invest the Lord's money. I carefully analyzed the ramifications and potential profits of managing a Kool-Aid stand but wasn't impressed by the expected net earnings. Then I heard of a nanny goat for sale. Clearly, a goat dairy would be a sensible—if not ingenious—money-making business. With only a small initial investment, virtually limitless profits would return to me. It was the perfect plan: buyers would get a perpetual supply of milk, God would get the money, and I— well, I would get the glory.

At the farm I looked over the goat with critical scrutiny, not wanting to buy a bum goat. She was pure white and had a long, curly beard dangling from her chin. Her long, serene face was adorned with a pointy nose and floppy ears. Her thin legs and bony knees were contrasted by a well-rounded belly, and, I noted with satisfaction, her udder looked ready to burst. She was absolutely beautiful in all of her white glory (nobody had ever told me the devil can appear as an angel of light). I knew I had found the perfect goat for my building-fund dairy—and at what a price!

I smugly handed the farmer my silver dollar, pleased with the excellent deal I had made in the bargaining, and was given fifty cents in change. In retrospect, I should have wondered at the pleased smile of relief on the farmer's face as we loaded the goat into our battered station wagon and headed home. She seemed docile and even friendly. Peace filled my heart, knowing all would go as planned. After all, I was on the Lord's errand.

When on the Lord's errand, tears of joy might be expected. I, on the other hand, could come up only with tears of anger and frustration—and plenty of them. I had never milked a goat before, and my first attempts were a disaster. Being nearly twice my size, she took advantage of my attempts to milk her. She jumped, kicked, and bucked with such fervor that I knew she had to be possessed by the devil. And all I had to show for my strenuous efforts were grass stains, bruises, and sore hands.

She was insidiously pleasant when the milk bucket was out of sight and I wasn't trying to milk her, but as soon as she saw me coming with milk bucket in hand, she rolled her eyes back and bared her yellow teeth in stubborn, wicked defiance. I knew she had resolved never to let me milk her and make my life as miserable as possible.

My dad bought me a milking stall to help me out, but even this proved no match for a goat possessing strength greater than nature had intended. Not only was it a great wrestling struggle between boy and beast to get her into the stall, but once she was in and I started to milk, she still managed to kick the bucket over or step in the hard-earned milk with a manure-covered hoof. I was beaten down and extremely discouraged. Not only had I failed at getting enough milk to sell, I was also getting weary of trudging out every morning and night to feed and water her.

With careful shrewdness I devised an intricate plan to rid my life of this cursed goat. This clever scheme, employed on my dad, consisted of incessant whining. My plan might as well have been used on an oak tree—it had about the same effect. His solution to the problem was to tie her legs to the stall so I could milk her without fear for my life. I was finally able to get enough milk to sell!

Luckily, Jewel McDermont, a widow lady down the road, couldn't drink cow's milk and could stand the taste of the (in my opinion, foul) goat's milk. Jewel was a nice old lady but seemed to enjoy hiding that fact with a sour expression and a harsh, demanding voice. Every couple days I delivered to her a quart of the hard-earned milk.

I wish I could remember how much the widow paid for the milk or how much money I actually ended up giving the branch president. I'm sure my monetary contribution to the building fund was small and trivial, but somehow the dividends paid to my soul have been priceless. A sense of commitment to the Lord's Church was gained, the seeds of a testimony were planted, and the great feeling that comes from sacrificing to serve the Lord were all instilled in me.

The Primary chorister was teaching the children the lyrics "The golden plates lay hidden deep in a mountain side, until God found one faithful, in whom he could confide." The chorister then asked, "Who was the one faithful, in whom God could confide?"

Matt raised his hand excitedly until he was called on. He then responded proudly, "It was me!"

—Brad Wilcox

Wash Away Sins

KENT STEPHENS

Several years ago it was time for my grandson to be baptized. There were other children in his ward who were also going to be baptized that same day. The bishop asked my grandson if it mattered whether he was baptized first, second, or last.

He responded that he wanted to be baptized first so that he would not get the sins left over in the water from the children who would be baptized before him.

It's Sometimes Hard to Say No

STEPHANIE JENSON

It was the 4th of July and a Sunday. My husband was substituting in Primary. Our fourteen-year-old son came up to his dad just as the kids were going to class. Our son asked if he could skip sacrament meeting and go on a picnic with one of the families in the ward. My husband told him no, but our boy continued to beg. He is a very persuasive kid and nearly prevailed, but in the end Dad stood firm.

When my husband got to class, his lesson was about choosing the right and how hard it sometimes is to say no.

One of the children raised his hand and said, "You even have a hard time saying no sometimes, don't you Brother Jenson? I heard you talking to your son, and it was hard for you to say no, wasn't it?"

What if he had told our son yes? We never know when these sweet children are watching us. We must always remember to be a good example.

Heidi Loves the Sacrament

BECKIE W. KEARL

My daughter Heidi loves the sacrament. That always impresses our family because she doesn't like to eat bread or drink water. Heidi was born with a serious physical problem called cerebral palsy. She can't hear or talk. She can't sit up alone or walk. She can use her hands only very awkwardly.

Her mouth and stomach muscles are so tight that eating hurts, and she has always hated it. She gets fed through a tube in her stomach while she sleeps at night.

We offer her food when we're eating, but nine times out of ten she will shake her head no and tightly shut her mouth. Even on her birthdays, when we have cheesecake—her favorite—she usually refuses to eat it. I help her hold a spoon and scoop up some of the cheesecake. Heidi smiles the whole time. But when I try to get it to her mouth, Heidi frowns and pushes the spoon toward my mouth and feeds me the cheesecake instead.

But in Heidi's twelve years of life, I have never once seen her frown or close her mouth to the sacrament. We've tried giving her little pieces of bread and sips of water at other times, but she'll never take them.

It has taken me a while to figure out this mystery, but I think I finally have. Heidi likes the sacrament because it isn't just food. Since she can't talk, it's hard for me to know how much she knows about Jesus Christ. I don't know if she understands that he was born in a stable or that he died on the cross. I guess for Heidi that doesn't really matter. What is important for her to know about Jesus Christ, Heidi understands. She knows she needs this bread and water in her life. I wish you could see her smile when she takes the sacrament.

I don't take the sacrament for granted, thanks to my daughter Heidi. I know I need it too.

Note: Shortly after this story was written, Heidi died from complications due to her cerebral palsy. The way she attempted to take the sacrament was a miracle to all around her, and we wanted to share it with you.

I'll Soon Be Eight

GENEVA FACEMYER

I'll soon be eight.
I think that's great.
I'll be just like the big guys—
Not big in size,
Not big and wise,
Just big enough to be baptized.

We attended cousin Joey's baptism. When Uncle Bob and Joey entered the font, two-year-old David caused quite a stir, blurting out, "Why are they going swimming with their clothes on?"

—Brad Wilcox

I Love to See the Temple

FIONA HOWELL

When my son Jonathan was four years old, he loved singing. He would sing to me and my husband all the time. He often put on performances for us on his bed, on chairs, anywhere he felt he could provide his entertainment.

One night he was standing on our coffee table in the living room asking for requests. We requested a family favorite, "I Love to See the Temple."

At the top of his voice, he sang, "For the temple is a house of God, a place of love and beauty. I'll 'repair' myself while I am young . . ."

At the time we thought it was funny how he mixed up the word repair for prepare, but my mother reminded me that not only do we need to prepare ourselves to enter the house of the Lord, in some cases we also need to repair ourselves. The Lord has given us the law of repentance to do just that, repair ourselves so we may receive his blessings, including those of the temple.

A Primary teacher was discussing the Ten Commandments with her six-year-olds. After explaining the commandment to "honor thy father and thy mother," she asked, "Is there a commandment that teaches us how to treat our brothers and sisters?"

One little boy (the oldest of a family of seven) answered, "Thou shall not kill."

—David Strahan

The Confession

MEL JONES

The day had been long, and I went straight to the bedroom to take off my tie and kick off my shoes. Through the open window I could hear my wife in the backyard chastising our two little boys for throwing rocks at the kids next door.

I sank down onto the bed to untie my shoes and suddenly had that feeling that parents get when something is not quite right with the kids. I looked out the window in time to see eight-year-old Chad leading his six-year-old brother in a sneak attack, their baby sister toddling along behind. They crept up to the fence, launched their rocks, and then scrambled back, delighted with their cunning strike.

"Chad! Shawn!" My words hit them like a voice of doom. Guilt crept over their two little faces as extra ammunition slipped from now limp fingers. "Come into the house now."

I sat back down on the bed and assumed my most judicial posture. There was a timid knock on the bedroom door. "Come in, boys." The tone of my voice portended terrible consequences.

The two boys shuffled in, eyes glued to the floor. I almost smiled, remembering a similar situation when I was the little one looking up at my dad. The memory softened my heart.

We discussed the terrible things that could result from throwing rocks. I ended by saying, "But the worst part of it all is the fact that you deliberately disobeyed your mother!" Both were speechless.

"Go to your room and make a list of ten reasons why we should never throw rocks and what can happen when we do. In a few minutes I will be in to check your list." As they left I gave each a sturdy pat on the rear to let them know I really was unhappy with them.

As they left, I went back to removing my shoes and unbuttoning my shirt, hardly conscious of the little angel standing by the corner of the bed.

"Dad-Dad, me throw rocks, too." I turned to her and almost laughed at the thought of my tiny two-year-old throwing rocks more than a few inches. However, the tears welling up in those little blue eyes convinced me that she was serious.

In a most grave tone I asked, "Did you throw rocks, too?" The baby blues overflowed as the little head slowly bobbed up and down. I gathered her into my arms, but she insisted on being returned to the floor. Through her sobs she muttered, "Pank, Dad-Dad," and leaned over my knee.

I was overwhelmed by the strong sense of justice that impelled this little angel to insist upon the consequences of her actions. The thump which I administered to that little diaper might have wounded but never could have killed a mosquito—but it was enough. Having confessed her sin, she could now accept the love and hugs, which I administered most liberally.

Now I was prepared to go in and review the boys' list, having been superbly instructed on the need for confession by a two-year-old.

One Sunday morning when my daughter was five years old, we were running a little behind, which was not uncommon in our family of five. As I rushed to get everyone ready for church, I saw my daughter playing instead of brushing her teeth. "Hurry, sweetie," I said. "You really need to hurry and get ready!"

She dropped everything, covered her face with her hands, and moaned, "Oh no! Is it fast Sunday again?"

—Stacey Reese

"You Don't Have the Priesthood Yet"

YOLANDA DIXON

When my boys were younger, they had an unusually direct way of applying the knowledge they were learning in church. This lead to some unfortunate, though humorous, applications of gospel principles.

I remember when my two oldest, still very young and able to bathe together, were making noise in the bathroom. To my surprise, I heard the older son raise his voice to his younger brother, who rarely ever upset his older brother. When I heard what the older son was complaining about, however, I understood. He was saying, "Hey! Cut that out! You don't have the priesthood yet!" The younger son was attempting to baptize him.

Giving Credit Where Credit Is Due

MARSHA HUGHES

When we were growing up our dad was always trying new things. One year he decided to get into bee-keeping and was very enthusiastic about everything he was learning. When the time finally came to reap honey from the bees, he took all of us out to the truck, where he showed us his first beautiful squares of honeycomb. Well, he was really bragging about what he had done, when our little sister looked at him innocently and said, "Dad, Jesus made the bees, and the bees made the honey!" He said that brought him down a peg or two. We still laugh at the sweet faith of this little girl who gave credit where credit was due.

Birth, Death, and Resurrection

To Live with Father in Heaven

ROD BOSS

Our youngest daughter, Miriem, was selected to be the "little sister" of a make-believe family in the Primary program in sacrament meeting. The family was to discuss the plan of salvation as if they were in a family home evening. Three-year-old Miriem was very excited about being part of the program but was a little nervous.

When asked by the mother what she should do in order to live again with her Father in Heaven, she was to answer, "Obey the commandments." We practiced over and over, and she became very confident. The day of the program finally came, and she sat very proudly on the stand. As the program began I noticed that Miriem was extremely attentive to what the others were saying about the plan of salvation. This seemed a little unusual because she, being so young, was normally restless during our meetings. Finally her part came, and I silently prayed that she would do a good job. The mother turned to her and said, "Miriem, what should we do in order to return to live with our Father in Heaven?"

There was a slight pause as Miriem looked down for a moment, and then she looked the mother in the eye and confidently said, "Die." The stunned mother and others were silent for some time, and the congregation chuckled when they realized this was not in the script. The mother recovered and quickly added that there were also things we could do here to prepare to return to our Father in Heaven.

This experience taught me that we should not underestimate our children's capacity to understand gospel principles, even at a very young age.

One Monday my wife gave the family home evening lesson about how in the premortal existence we chose to come to earth and live in families. Later that evening, when I was summoned by the cries of our six-month-old daughter, I heard my six-year-old son, who was standing by her crib and patting her back, say, "Don't cry, you're the one who wanted to come here."

—Anonymous

Born Here

BRAD WILCOX

My wife works part time at a same-day surgery unit of a local hospital. One day she was sitting outside on a bench and enjoying her lunch when a little boy—about seven years old—came riding up on his bike. Seeing that she was in a nurse's uniform, he stopped and said, "Hi! You remember me?"

My wife studied him and said, "Give me a second here."

The boy's smile faded. He asked again, "You don't remember me?"

My wife tried desperately to place his face. Finally, she admitted, "I'm sorry. Where would I know you from?"

To this the boy responded, "I was born here."

Repairing Grandpa

ROBERT P. BARNES

Years ago, while living in Arizona, we owned an old yellow cat. We sort of inherited the cat when we moved into the home (i.e., he allowed us to share his home), and he became good friends with our young son Jon, who was five or six years old at the time.

A year or two after we moved in, the cat became ill, and my wife took him to the vet. When the examination was completed, the doctor informed us that the cat had a serious urinary tract infection that rendered it impossible to pass anything through the urinary tract. The doctor gave us three options:

1) a $150 operation that might fix the problem (odds were 50-50),
2) a $295 operation that might fix the problem (odds were 80-20), or
3) a $17.95 operation that would fix the problem (odds were 100 percent—the cat would be put to sleep).

After explaining the situation to Jon, we all agreed that we couldn't afford the more expensive options and elected the $17.95 solution. Although he was disappointed, Jon seemed to take it pretty well, and we closed that chapter.

A year or so later we received a call from my father, Grandpa Bob, who lived in Salt Lake City. He explained that he was going into the hospital the next day for some tests and, possibly, an operation. He said he had prostate problems, and when Jon asked him what that meant, he explained that it made it difficult to go to the bathroom. We talked with him for a while, wished him good luck, and then hung up the phone, promising to check in the next night to see how things were going. After we hung up, I looked at Jon and saw that he had large tears running down his face.

I asked him what was wrong, and he said, "Do you think Grandpa is worth saving?"

The minds of young children are so innocent and humble. It's no wonder we are counseled to be more like them.

The Age of a Tree

LORI SMITH

Soon after my son, Scott, turned five years old, we were attending a baptism. While the new convert was dressing, Scott was drawing. When he had finished scribbling on the paper, Scott decided he wanted to keep the paper for plans to build a tree house. He asked me in a soft whisper if he could have a tree house. I explained that we didn't have a tree strong enough to support a tree house. He countered with the idea that we could plant one.

I replied, "By the time the tree grew big enough and strong enough to put a tree house in it, you'd be an old man ready to die."

Without a moment of hesitation, he said, "That's okay! We'll come finish it after the resurrection, okay Mommy?"

Burying Fred

ELYSSA RENEE ANDRUS

In my house, packing is a polite term for war. Getting eleven people ready for a family vacation is hard, and the hours before departure are usually sheer mayhem. One year, before we left for San Diego, we were having a particularly hard time getting ourselves together. Mom, eight months pregnant, hid in the kitchen stuffing M&Ms into Ziplock bags and her mouth. I think she hoped the older kids would pack for her. Dad, having dropped off Rico Suave and Fred, our two pet iguanas, at the neighbors, had finished his to-do list. He was lost. So he wandered around the house scattering papers and muttering to himself.

The kids were engaged in all-out battle. The older ones ran up and down the stairs yelling vague threats to the younger ones, who were diligently unpacking the suitcases. When the doorbell rang, my sister Katrina and I were tying six-year-old Jake to a chair with a jump rope to keep him from drawing more waves on the kitchen wall.

The doorbell chimed four times before someone answered it. When Dad opened it, our next-door neighbor Allison stood in the doorway quivering. In her hand she held several paper towels with a green tail poking out.

"It's Fred," she said.

Dad called for Steven.

"I think he's dead," Allison said as she offered Steven the small iguana corpse. "The heat must've gotten to him."

Steven went through the grieving stages quickly, grabbing his pet and screaming, "Not Fred, not Fred, not Fred!" The family came running. Dad took Steven, who at ten was not a small child, in his arms and carried him into the study. Mom, crying almost as hard as Steven, tried to direct us back to packing.

Dad and Steven emerged from the study an hour later, Dad's gigantic hand clutching Steven's small, chubby one. Steven's eyes were dark red from crying, but he seemed somewhat stable. He asked for help with the funeral. For a coffin he chose a black box from the mountain of shoe boxes in my closet, and we lined it with pink sheets pilfered from an old Barbie Dream House. Steven asked Jared, who was four years older and also had an iguana, to be a pallbearer for the procession. We marched silently, a mob of children behind a shoe box casket, to the west side of our front yard to bury Fred.

We began with an opening prayer. Since Jake, the youngest, was territorial about prayer, he said every blessing at our house. "Dear Heavenly Father," he said. "Thank you for this day. Bless Fred. Bless Steven. And please bless the food to nurse and straiten our body." Even Steven had to suppress a giggle.

We tried to sing "Amazing Grace," but no one knew what came after "a wretch like me." We sang "Families Can Be Together Forever" instead. Steven delivered the eulogy. "Fred was a good iguana. She never bit anyone and ate all her carrots and lettuce. She liked to play on her tree, and she hardly ever wet on me. She'd fall asleep on my arm," he said. He started crying hard. Tears covered his fat cheeks. He rubbed them away with dirty hands. "I loved her," he blubbered.

"Steven, it will be all right," Dad said as he put his arm on Steven's shoulder. "Remember what we talked about? Come on, why don't you be the one to dig the grave?"

"Okay, I know, Dad, I know," said Steven, taking deep, heaving breaths to stop crying. He took out a gardening shovel and struck at the earth, sending dust everywhere. The Tucson sun beat down; I noticed sweat beading on my father's forehead. We shifted uncomfortably, sadly, as the locusts buzzed in the background. "How much longer, Mom?" asked Jake, pulling on my mother's pant legs. Finally, Steven finished and lowered the shoe box into the earth. He knelt to fill the hole with dirt and cover the grave.

As he did so, Rebecca—the child just older than Jake—burst into a song, which she made up as she sang. "Oh Frrrrred, we loved you and we will miss you, our good iguana Frrrred, our good iguana Frrrrred," she sang. After several rambling verses Dad looked over at Mom, who was slumped over on me for support, and decided he had had enough. "Thank you, Rebecca," he said. "We will now have a closing prayer by Jake and reconvene in the house to finish packing."

Jake prayed again, and as we turned to leave, Steven stopped us. "Wait, guys, one second," he said shyly and reached in his pocket. He produced a headstone, which he had made from a chipped granite rock. On its face, in small uneven letters written in black marker, it read:

Here lies Fred
Born Christmas 1994
Died July 10, 1996

There was a large epitaph at the bottom which read:

"I'll be back!"

The kids began to giggle. Dad and Mom smiled at each other. Steven, already flushed from the heat, turned a shade redder. He looked up at Dad and said, "Just like we talked about, Dad."

Dad smiled in wonder, finding himself the student. Steven's faith in the resurrection was simple, absolute. I felt my eyes wet as I thought of my younger brother saying good-bye to his iguana, never questioning that someday he would see him again. Fred would be back. Steven laid the headstone down, took a deep breath, and walked back toward the house.

"You're right, son, just like we talked about," Dad said to himself, watching Steven. Dad smiled the whole day.

My mother tells of a time when I was asked to pick my favorite Primary song for singing time. "Let's sing the resurrection song," I suggested after some thought. Baffled, the Primary chorister asked, "What's the resurrection song?"

"You know," came my reply as I began to sing, "'My body lies over the ocean, my body lies over the sea. My body lies over the ocean, oh bring back my body to me'!"

—Trisha Dixon

A Potato Bug Reunion

MICHAELENE P. GRASSLI

Sue's three-year-old grandson, Trent, was visiting. As they were playing outside, he started stomping on some potato bugs. Sue called him to her and explained about reverence for life. "Those potato bugs were some potato bug's children," she said, "or some bug's mother and dad or grandma and grandpa." She explained that the other bugs would miss them if Trent kept stamping on them and killing them. He looked very solemnly at her and listened carefully. She thought she had solved the problem, teaching him a most significant lesson. The next time she turned around she saw him stomping even more vigorously on potato bugs. Sue was dismayed and said, "Trent, I thought we had a talk about that."

Trent said, "It's okay, Grandma, because I'm going to get them all and then all the families can be together forever in heaven."

Simple Faith

JULIANN DOMAN

I had just started my new job working with four-year-olds. I was part of a government team trying to give children a "head start" before they began school. Many of the children enrolled in the program came from families with little money, and some had limited physical abilities as well. I was hired as a speech therapist aide, so my job consisted of interacting, talking, and mostly listening to the children.

One day I observed a precious interchange between two friends who were making bracelets for each other.

One little girl remarked, "I'm making a heart bracelet for you!" which she eagerly showed her friend.

The teacher, who stood nearby, then commented, "That must mean you love your friend."

The girl replied matter-of-factly, "Well, Jesus loves everyone. He died for us."

Her friend then wisely added, "Yes, but now he's alive again."

There, in that busy room full of four-year-olds, I felt what a blessing it was to be among children who were sharing with me their simple faith.

It was obvious that little Katie had received too many object lessons when she was asked in Primary why we came to earth and she responded, "We came to get our glove."

—Debbie Heath

The Will of the Lord

MARBA C. JOSEPHSON

Faith has always been the fundamental characteristic of Lucy ["Lutie"] G. Cannon. From the earliest childhood, the Lord has manifested himself in her behalf. When she was about twelve years of age, her mother died. When her father [President Heber J. Grant] told Lucy that her mother was dying, Lucy would not believe him. She hurried from the room and returned with a bottle of consecrated oil and implored him to bless her mother. [President Grant] blessed his wife, dedicating her to the Lord. As the children left the room, he fell on his knees and prayed that his wife's death might not affect the faith of their children in the ordinances of the Gospel. "Lutie" herself ran from the house feeling very bad, as she expressed in the following words:

"I was stunned and shocked and felt my father had not sufficient faith. I went behind the house and knelt

173

down and prayed for the restoration of my mother. Instantly a voice, not an audible one, but one that seemed to speak to my whole being, said, 'In the death of your mother the will of the Lord will be done.' Immediately I was a changed child. I felt reconciled and happy."

My four-year-old grandson anxiously awaited his first day in preschool. His teacher had given the assignment for all the children to bring something that made them special to display at show and tell. When asked by his mom the night before what he wanted to take, my grandson, who was adopted, proudly announced that he was going to take the book *Tell Me about the Night I Was Born*, because being adopted made him special.

—Carolyn Olsen

Prayer

"Nothing Will Hurt You"

DAVID O. McKAY

When a very young child in the home of my youth, I was fearful at night. I traced it back to a vivid dream in which two Indians came into the yard. I ran to the house for protection, and one of them shot an arrow and hit me in the back. Only a dream, but I felt that blow, and I was very much frightened, for in the dream they entered [the house], . . . a tall one, and a smaller one, and sneered and frightened Mother.

I never got over it. Added to that were the fears of my mother, for when Father was away with the herd, or on some mission, Mother would never retire without looking under the bed; so burglars or men who might enter the house and try to take advantage of Mother and the young children were real to me.

Whatever the conditions, I was very much frightened. One night I could not sleep, and I fancied I heard noises around the house. Mother was away in another room.

Thomas E. by my side was sleeping soundly. I became terribly wrought in my feeling, and I decided to pray as my parents had taught me.

I thought I could pray only by getting out of bed and kneeling, and that was a terrible test. But I did finally bring myself to get out of bed and kneel and pray to God to protect Mother and the family. And a voice, [speaking] as clearly to me as mine is to you, said, "Don't be afraid. Nothing will hurt you." Where it came from, what it was, I am not saying. You may judge. To me it was a direct answer.

It was my little girl's first chance to receive a father's blessing, and I thought I had prepared her well. However, I soon realized there were still a few things she needed to know. When I placed my hands on her head and said, "Whitney Wilcox . . . ," she interrupted and asked, "What?"

—Brad Wilcox

An Unusual Answer

LINDA TENNEY

We have enjoyed having our son and daughter-in-law and their two sons, Tyson, age five, and Jacson, age two, live in our home for the past ten months. A few Sundays ago, our Gospel Doctrine teacher told us that when children have challenges and problems parents should encourage them to go to Heavenly Father in prayer for guidance and answers instead of always trying to give them the answers themselves. This way children learn the principle of relying on the Spirit.

An opportunity to apply this principle presented itself that very afternoon. Tyson became angry with his younger brother, Jacson, and threw a toy at him. Tad and Dianna, his parents, told him about their lesson in Sunday School and invited him to go into his bedroom and pray about what he had just done. Tyson obeyed and closed the door behind him.

A few minutes later Tyson came out and reported, "Heavenly Father said I do not have to say sorry to Jacson. He also said I do not have to eat peas anymore."

One evening we were just about to have dinner. It was the first time my wife had prepared this particular dish, and we were all looking at her new delicacy, not quite sure what we should do with it. Anyway, it was our five-year-old son Joshua's turn to give the prayer. I said, "Go ahead and say the prayer, Joshua." He paused, bowed his head, and prayed, "Dear Heavenly Father, please help us eat this stuff, even though we don't like it, so Mom won't be mad."

—Curtis L. Jacobs

From *Feeling Great, Doing Right, Hanging Tough: Favorite Talks from Especially for Youth*, 1991, 47.

"How About Your Prayers?"

ROBERT L. SIMPSON

It was thrilling to listen to a father relate this story about his three-year-old youngster recently, as they knelt by the crib in the usual manner for the little fellow to say his simple bedtime prayer. Eyes closed—heads bowed—seconds passed, and there were no words spoken by the child. Just about the time Dad was going to open his eyes to check the lengthy delay, little Tommy was on his feet and climbing into bed.

"How about your prayers?" asked Dad.

"I said my prayers," came the reply.

"But son, Daddy didn't hear you."

Then followed the child's classic statement: "But Daddy, I wasn't talking to you."

"Doctor, Won't You Pray for Me?"

GEORGE ALBERT SMITH

A little boy was upon the operating table, ready to undergo an operation for appendicitis—an orphan boy, about eight years of age. It was a rather unusual case, and by the way a charity case. As the boy lay there he looked up at the surgeons—there were several of them present—and addressing the surgeon in charge he said: "Doctor, before you begin to operate, won't you pray for me?" The surgeon looked at the boy amazed and said, "Why, I can't pray for you." Then the little fellow turned his eyes from one to the other, asking each if they would pray for him. Each in turn declined. Then the little man said: "If you won't pray for me, won't you please wait while I pray for myself?" The little fellow got up and on the operating table on his knees, folded his hands, and uttered a prayer. He said to the Lord:

"Heavenly Father, I am only a little orphan boy, but I am awful sick, and these doctors are going to operate. Will you please help them that they will do it right? And now, Heavenly Father, if you will make me well I will be a good boy. Thank you for making me well." He then turned over and laid on his back and looked up at the doctors and nurses who were all standing around, but he was the only one in the room who could see because the others had tears in their eyes. He said: "Now I am ready."

A few days after that a man went into the office of the chief surgeon and asked him to tell him the story of the little boy he had operated on a few days before. The surgeon said: "I have operated on a good many little boys."

"Yes, I know, but this was an unusual case—tell me about it."

Then the doctor looked at him for some time and said, "I don't know whether I will tell you or not. I am not sure but what it is too sacred to talk about."

"Please tell me," he replied; "I will treat it as sacred, too." Then the doctor told the story as I have related it, and when he got through the visitor said, "My, that was a remarkable experience, wasn't it?"

The doctor said, "Remarkable? That was the most remarkable experience of my whole life. I have operated on hundreds of men, women, and children, and I have known some of them to pray, but never until I stood in the presence of that little boy, have I heard anyone talk to their Heavenly Father face to face."

"But What Should I Say, Daddy?"

RON MATHES

I was helping my young son Craig with his prayers one evening. Kneeling with him at his bedside, I explained to him that he should talk openly to Heavenly Father, thank Him for whatever he felt thankful for, ask Heavenly Father for blessings for himself and for others, and then close his prayer. Craig said, "But what should I say, Dad?" Not wanting him to become repetitious in his prayers, I said, "Just tell Him what's in your heart."

Craig was satisfied with that and then proceeded with "Dear Heavenly Father, I've got blood in my heart." The rest of the prayer was just fine.

"For of Such Is the Kingdom of God"

CINDY COLLYER

I grew up in a family in which we teased one another a great deal. I later carried my enjoyment of teasing into my relationship with my husband and children. I remember one occasion some twenty years ago when I took my teasing too far.

My husband and I and our two little children were living in suburban San Antonio, Texas. Whenever we went to church, the grocery store, or almost anywhere, we had to pass through some rural wooded areas. One day not long after I had introduced my kids to the story "Hansel and Gretel," my children and I were driving through one of these areas. I suggested that I might leave them in this wooded area with some bread to see if they could find their way home. My daughter, Callie, was five or six years old at the time. I didn't realize how terribly my comment had frightened her until she came to me one morning, a day or two later.

"Mommy," she said, "last night Heavenly Father told me not to worry about you leaving me in the forest. He told me you were just kidding me."

How grateful I am that Heavenly Father intervened to reassure this little child after I had been so careless. Throughout my life I have often prayed, and I continue to pray, that through the Savior's wonderful Atonement, Heavenly Father will compensate my children where I have fallen short as a parent.

I said a quick blessing on the food because everyone was especially hungry. As I concluded Whitney was disgusted. She said, "That was a bad prayer! You didn't say Grandma or Grandpa or missionaries or prophet! That was a bad prayer!"

—Brad Wilcox

A Prayer for Bobby

MICHAELENE P. GRASSLI

Bobby, a six-year-old boy with a disfigured face, visited in a Primary class taught by a friend of mine. He came in and sat, body trembling, in the opening exercises. In class, the teacher introduced the frightened little boy by name to the regular members of the class and then asked Lynda to give the prayer. In the prayer Lynda, unprompted, thanked Heavenly Father that Bobby could be in Primary with them that day. Following the prayer the teacher noticed that Bobby was no longer trembling, that he sat a little straighter, that he seemed not to be frightened. He participated in class, although he suffered from a severe speech impediment. Lynda's tender, sensitive prayer had brought an unusually strong spirit into the class that day. After Primary, the little boy hugged the teacher and said, "Oh, I like this Primary best of all."

"And Please Bless..."

MATTHEW O. RICHARDSON

Some of my most memorable and enjoyable experiences have been kneeling with my children at their bedsides in prayer. One evening while praying with Megan, I listened carefully as she calmly went through her agenda. For a while it seemed as if she were going to bless everyone and everything. I marveled at her patience. She wasn't in a hurry, and her words were sincere and straightforward. She had already mentioned each sibling, my wife, me, and most of the extended family, and then she paused. I guess I noticed the pause because it was so rare. Megan typically began with "Dear Heavenly Father" and spoke in a steady stream of words straight through to her concluding "amen."

I peeked at Megan only to find her arms still folded and her eyes clenched shut. Then she said calmly, "And please bless Satan . . ."

Please bless Satan? I thought. *Can you say that?* After

another short pause, she finished her unusual request, ". . . so that he will get better."

I was moved by Megan's compassion and unconditional love—even for Satan. I don't know whether her petition could soften a heart as hard as his, but it was encouraging as a father to see such pure faith and compassion in my daughter.

One night I went up to tuck my seven- and nine-year-old daughters in bed. When I got upstairs, the light was off and the younger daughter, Michelle, was on her knees saying her nightly prayers. Rebecca was lying on her own bed and was making a series of tones with her mouth. I looked over at her and made a quiet shushing sound to get her to be quiet while her sister was praying. She responded by saying, "I'm calling Michelle on the phone." Michelle then looked up and responded, "I'm saying my prayers. Leave a message!"

—Anonymous

A Sister in a Storm

KATHY FORD

Thunderstorms are all too common where we live in the Midwest. As we visited another ward for fast and testimony meeting on the morning after a particularly long and loud storm, we heard many bear their testimonies of the beauty of the Lord's creations. Many had found beauty in the power of the storms. One sister, however, quietly walked to the pulpit and spoke of her terror of the bright flashes of lightning and loud claps of thunder. She told the congregation about how she had been abused as a child and been locked into a closet during one such storm. Her speech was impaired, and her mental capacity seemed somewhat limited as she spoke of things that most usually wouldn't share publicly.

During the following week, we experienced more electrical storms. I was riding in the car with my daughter one day after such a storm. She asked if I remembered the woman who had borne her testimony and had talked about being afraid of the storms.

I said, "Yes, I do remember her. Wasn't she a little strange?"

But my daughter didn't answer my question. "I was worried that she was alone and afraid during the storm last night," she replied, "so I prayed for her!"

I instantly felt regret for my answer. How had I missed what was there for all the world to see? My daughter was an example to me of Christlike love. She had heard a message to which I had closed my ears. Her simple statement made me see past this sister's mental limitations and feel the pain and fear that were in her heart as she bore such an intimate testimony.

Michael's Prayer

MICHAELENE P. GRASSLI

Four-year-old Michael was playing at a friend's home. His eighteen-month-old sister, Marlies, was there too, and, as eighteen-month-olds often do, she had grabbed and bothered until Michael's patience was sorely tested. At lunch, as Michael offered the blessing, he interjected, "Heavenly Father, please take Marlies for just a little while so she won't ruin our Lego setup."

Heavenly Father could do anything. Surely he could just "tend" the baby and keep her out of the way temporarily.

"The Wind Has Gone Down!"

SOPHY H. VALENTINE

I often think of an incident that occurred in my childhood [in the 1860s and early 1870s] and gave me great comfort to dwell upon.

I was then living with my aunt in Wisconsin on a big farm three or four miles from Racine. I had no playmates of my own age. I received private instruction three times a week by the Danish clergyman, so I did not even have the pleasure and exhilaration of school life. I was far away from my dear home and was often very lonely. I had, however, one friend, a girl of my own age, who lived four miles farther out in the country. To her I was very much attached, and at her home I spent my happiest days.

It was on my birthday, the 12th of February. I had been promised that I should be allowed to spend two days at my friend's and I had looked forward to this for weeks; I had drowned many a little grief in the hope of this pleasure.

Well, the day dawned at last and I awoke by hearing the limbs of the apple tree beat violently against the window shutters. My heart sank within me, for I knew that with this terrific windstorm and the thermometer ten degrees below zero, I would not be permitted to go.

All morning I went about with a tearful face, looking despairingly out of the window for a sign of some encouragement in the look of the weather, but the wind kept up its terrible howl and shook the trees till many of them broke. Aunty scolded me for my despondent looks and told me to give it up, as there was no hope of the wind going down from the looks of things.

I went up in the front room and stood shivering with cold, chewing my apron in deepest despair and trying to check the deep sobbing that shook me. Then in my sorrow I dropped on my knees and cried imploringly to the Lord to have pity on me and my loneliness; to let the wind go down that I might go. I ended my prayer by reminding him how Jesus had promised that we should receive whatsoever we asked in his name. Full of faith and courage, I arose and went to the window. The trees shook as if some mighty hand had hold of them, and then suddenly let go. I stood and stared, not daring to breathe. The trees swayed softly to and fro and finally made not a move. I knelt again and whispered a hurried, excited, thanks dear Lord, and then flew into the sitting room. "Aunty! The wind has gone down!"

"No?"

"It has!"

Aunty went to the door and looked out and then exclaimed, "Well, I declare, so it has—I never saw anything like it." I went to my friend's house, of course.

Now, call it childishness if you like, or chance or anything, but it will not rob me of the pleasure I find in putting my own interpretation on it.

If I live to be an old, old woman I shall never forget it. I always thank the Lord, who remembered the poor lonely child though she was not then a member of The Church of Jesus Christ of Latter-day Saints. It shows to me that God is interested in the everyday affairs of his children.

Faith of a Child

HEBER C. KIMBALL

My wife, one day, when going out on a visit, gave my daughter Helen Mar charge not to touch the dishes, for if she broke any during her absence she would give her a whipping when she returned. While my wife was absent my daughter broke a number of the dishes by letting the table leaf fall, and then she went out under an apple tree and prayed that her mother's heart might be softened, that when she returned she might not whip her. Her mother was very punctual when she made a promise to her children, to fulfill it, and when she returned she undertook, as a duty, to carry this promise into effect. She retired with her into her room, but found herself powerless to chastise her; her heart was so softened that it was impossible for her to raise her hand against the child. Afterwards, Helen told her mother she had prayed to the Lord that she might not whip her.

Love
and
Service

Love Thy Neighbor

ARDETH GREENE KAPP

One day I . . . was in a second grade elementary classroom. The student-teacher held the children captive with her storytelling skills. In great detail she told of a cross old man whose name was Mr. Black. In contrast, the account was given . . . of a Mr. Brown who was kind and thoughtful and loved by everyone. At the conclusion of the story, the teacher asked the children, "How many of you would like to be a neighbor to Mr. Brown?" Every hand was raised high. Then, almost as an afterthought, she inquired if there was anyone who would like to have Mr. Black for a neighbor.

A little boy in a faded green shirt near the back of the room began to raise his hand, which brought a ripple of quiet amusement from the children. When called on for an explanation to his single vote, he spoke in a soft tone. "Well," he said, "I'd like Mr. Black to be my neighbor, because if he was, my mom would make a cake for me

199

to take to him, and then he wouldn't be that way any-more." A hush fell over the room. Everyone felt some-thing wonderful that they couldn't explain. A little child broke the silence like a benediction: "Oh, I wish I'd said that!"

Our five-year-old daughter has quite a sweet rela-tionship with my sister—the favorite aunt. For nearly two years now, whenever the child speaks to her or about her, including in her prayers, she calls her "Beloved Aunt."

—Rebecca Chambers

"I Didn't Want You to Be Alone"

MICHAELENE P. GRASSLI

It was fast Sunday. My husband bore his testimony, commenting that he was alone that day due to my being away on a Church assignment. As he concluded his testimony and sat down, eight-year-old Torri, the youngest daughter in a family of six children, bounced out of her seat and slipped into the row where Leonard was sitting. She sat down next to him, put both arms around his waist, gave him a big hug, then sat there cuddled next to him with his arm around her. She whispered, "I didn't want you to be alone."

"Daddy, Why Do You Love Me?"

SCOTT SATTERFIELD

Some years ago my wife and my children's mother decided that she would use her agency and create a new life for herself without us. It left us all sad and hurting, but with the help of extended family members we didn't give up. These events seemed to hurt my son the most deeply, and he found it hard to believe that he was indeed loved. One day as I kissed and squeezed him and told him how I loved him, this six-year-old son of mine stopped, looked up into my eyes, and asked, "Daddy, why do you love me?"

I looked at him closely. I thought and considered that it was not for what he did or how he looked but for who he was. I answered, "I love you because you are mine!" That satisfied him, and he went about his normal six-year-old activities.

I, however, stood there for a moment and felt the significance of those words—an echo from on high. I felt

Heavenly Father's arms around me and knew of his love for me at a time when I wasn't sure anyone could love me. Were these children sent so that I could teach them, or are they here to teach me? I wonder every day.

Four-year-old Whitney taught her father quite a lesson when she sang her version of the lyrics to "I Am a Child of God." Innocently she sang, "Lead me, guide me, rock-a-bye me."

—Brad Wilcox

Angels in Camouflage

CORINA BURNER

One beautiful, clear day my son and I were on our way to help out with a Scout car wash. The sky was bright blue with billowy clouds—it was the perfect day. As we were driving down the road, my son made the comment, "Mom, I can see all the way to heaven." Puzzled, I replied, "You can?" He then answered, "Yeah, the angels are dressed in camouflage. You can't see them, but they're there."

I've reflected on his comment about the angels in camouflage many times. How profoundly true it is. For those angels dressed in camouflage often look just like you or me. We go through our lives, serving others, sometimes without realizing that we're making a difference. It's in those despairing moments of another that we become an "angel in camouflage" to them. We serve them, often not knowing their needs, but we come at precisely the moment they need our help. We may not know that our kind word, our gentle touch, or even a smile is just what they needed. But the Lord knows. As his children we truly become "angels in camouflage" when we serve one another.

As I was reading to our children one morning at breakfast, our eight-year-old beamed at me: "I like quality time with you, Mama, because it's also quantity time!"
—Rebecca Chambers

"Because He Loved Them"

SHANE DIXON

I stood at the door of a poorly constructed shack on a mountainside in Venezuela. We called this kind of house, made of tin walls and a dirt floor, a ranchito. Elder Johnson, my missionary companion, stood next to me and knocked lightly. The house shook from the slight force of his fist.

Several days earlier we had been stopped by the father of the family who resided in this shack. He was drunk and said that if we were really Christian we would "spend time with people like him who needed help." We agreed and had taught the family a discussion the next day. Now we were trying to have a follow-up visit, even though the father had seemed to regret his initial invitation. I was anxious to see the three little children, who had beamed as we sang Primary songs.

But no one answered the door. Just as we were about to leave, however, the three children bounded up the valley to reach the shack. The valley was a lush jungle of towering tropical trees with an underbelly of giant tree ferns. The three children seemed to rise from out of the jungle, conjuring images of castaways on a deserted island.

With great pride they had us sit down on boards and towels, which served as chairs. They sat on even cruder seats—bricks, a tin sheet, and a thermos. One little girl reminded us of our promise to sing "I Am a Child of God" again. As we sang the song, the children grinned. They offered to say the prayer (we had taught them how to pray in the first discussion), and the girl who served as voice asked God to help her learn how to read and to understand our message.

Afterward, as we were about to go, we asked if they had any more questions. The same girl said yes.

"Where do you live?" she asked, obviously aware of our accents and strange clothes.

"Not very far from here," we understated.

"Is it like this?"

"Yes, in some ways it is," we explained, trying to build on common ground. We shifted a little and explained some of the similarities of our homes and families. She responded as if she hadn't heard.

"So why are you here? If there it is so nice and here there is nothing, why do you want to be here, so far away?"

Surprised by the question, neither of us responded for a while. We looked at the dirt floor and the ugly ducks that walked past us. We saw the trash on the hillside and the dirty, mud-smeared smiles of the children. I realized that this girl had probably never even stepped into the wealthy parts of Caracas, even though the city was less than a half hour away. They stared at our white, ironed shirts and colorful ties, and I realized how different we seemed to them, regardless of our enthusiasm to show them otherwise. As they waited for an answer, I remembered the beautiful scripture Elder Johnson had shared with them about Jesus Christ.

"Do you remember when we spoke about how Christ went very far from his home to visit people in the Americas? How he lived across the sea but came here to heal the blind people and those that were sick?" They all nodded their heads affirmatively.

"And do you remember that he hugged and blessed all the children and even cried for them?" Again, they nodded. Then I asked the question I hoped would solve their inquiry.

"Now, why do you think he did all those things for the people who lived so far from his home?" Expecting that I would be the one to respond to my own question, I was startled when the little girl quickly answered, "Because he loved them."

A knot swelled in my throat as I silently considered her words. My mission would conclude in several weeks, and nothing seemed to sum up my feelings as well as what this young girl had said. I nodded to her quietly. My companion placed a hand on my shoulder, and we rose together off our seats. We shook hands with our small friends, and there was a final exchange of smiles. Thankful for a summary of my mission experience, I finally spoke, saying, "Well, I hope that's why we're here in Venezuela."

One day after dismissing my class of eight-year-olds, I noticed one student lingering. As soon as all the other students were gone, she approached me and said, "Teacher, I want to show you this card I made for McKenzie. Her independence burst and now she is in the hospital."

—Kathy Rees

Pacified

LINDA J. EYRE

Amidst the difficulty of life, seeing the humor in everyday living is often a mother's salvation. One mother wrote, "It was one of the worst days of my life. The washing machine broke down, the telephone kept ringing, my head ached, and the mail carrier brought a bill I had no money to pay. Almost to the breaking point, I lifted my one-year-old into his high chair, leaned my head against the tray, and began to cry. Without a word, my little son took his pacifier out of his mouth and stuck it in mine."

The Mean Man Next Door

ANGIE OLSON

I am a single mom with three children who at times can be a handful. Elizabeth, my youngest, is seven years old and may very well be the most mischievous child you'll ever meet. She's conniving and fun all at once. She's the one who frustrates us the most but who also keeps laughter in our home. She recently taught me about serving others through kindness.

As I got home Friday evening, April 30, I was greeted at the door by Elizabeth, who shared with me some May Day hanging art she had created in school. Ready to take it from her and hang it in the living room, she looked at me and said with conviction, "I'm going to give this to the man next door!" A little hurt by her desire to share with him and not me, I questioned her to make sure the man she was talking about was the man I was thinking about.

The neighborhood kids named our neighbor to the

east the "mean man." He spends a lot of time and money on his yard, and it is absolutely beautiful. If any child is caught in his yard, he threatens to call the police. He doesn't say anything to anyone and from what I've seen, doesn't smile. I verified with her that this indeed was the man she was speaking of. I thought to myself, *Let's see if she follows through on this one.*

The next morning was both May Day and Elizabeth's birthday. With so much excitement and lots of things to do, I really thought she'd forget about her plan. But as we headed out to take her brother to Scouts, she got into the car with the hymnbook (a hard surface to write on) and a plain piece of white paper for the note. We got very busy, and she was happy and thoughtful toward everyone all day.

After lunch she announced to me that she had done it. "I left it for him on his porch!" she said. "I didn't want to bother him, so I didn't even knock on the door. I wonder if he's found it and if he likes it."

The next morning I asked her about the note she'd delivered with her gift. Although somewhat reluctant to share it with me, she told me that the note simply said, "I love you, your neighbor." I have ever been grateful for her example to me. We now know almost all our neighbors, and we have discovered that the "mean man" next door isn't so mean after all.

Friends for Andre

MICHAELENE P. GRASSLI

As a Down's syndrome child, seven-year-old Andre had not had companions his age. His mother wanted him to be in a regular school so that he could have some friends to play with. The first-grade teachers prepared the class before Andre came the first day. They explained that he would need some help, that he needed friends, and that the children should be nice to him. The teachers thought it might be a good idea to assign buddies to Andre on a rotation basis so there would always be someone specific who could help him.

In the beginning the children wanted to "mother" Andre. They were so helpful that the buddy system wasn't necessary. The teachers even had to remind them that Andre needed to learn to do things for himself. As the year progressed, Andre did learn, and soon it was the children who were reminding the teachers that he could do things for himself.

In a March parent-teacher conference that year, Andre's mother wept in gratitude. She reported to his teacher that Andre had had his first invitation to a birthday party and that another child had actually invited him to stay overnight at his house. The unconditional love of those children was beyond what the teachers and parents had even hoped for.

A mother was teaching her little son about service. "We need to remember," she exclaimed, "that we're here on earth to help others."

The little boy looked puzzled. "But, Mommy," he asked, "Why are the others here?"

—From *Best-Loved Humor of the LDS People*,
ed. Linda Ririe Gundry, Jay A. Parry,
and Jack M. Lyon, 232.

Ears to Hear

PAULA HUNT

J ennifer had an indomitable spirit.

At church one day I told a visitor to move out of the way when Jennifer rushed by.

"Why?"

"Because she can't see you very well. You're just a shadow to her."

"That child is blind?" she asked, watching in amazement as Jennifer clattered fearlessly down the stairs.

Although cataracts and glaucoma had robbed Jennifer of most of her eyesight after a premature birth, Jennifer didn't know she should be handicapped by her lack of vision. Her zest for life wouldn't allow that.

When she was six, doctors told Jennifer she would lose the rest of her sight. Soon her shadowy world would turn completely black. Still, she learned to deal with her problems and continued life at full speed.

At school she made a special friend named Joseph,

who dealt with a hearing loss. Jennifer and Joseph studied together, often struggling through assignments by relying on the skills of the other. Eyes for ears, and ears for eyes.

One night as she was getting ready for bed, Jennifer turned to her mother, "Joseph can't hear when I read stories to him. I wish I could give him my ears. Then he could hear."

This touched her mother, and she took occasion to mention it to Joseph's mother. She looked surprised and replied, "Joseph said he was sad that Jennifer couldn't see. He wished he could give her his eyes."

A Turf War Averted

BARBARA B. SMITH

The power of love is generative.

I think my young son understood this when he was only three.

One morning I stepped to our back door to see the children off to school. Our little three-year-old son followed the children to the edge of the yard and watched them as they cut across the grass of a newly moved-in neighbor. Enraged, the neighbor called out, "Don't you kids ever cut across my lawn; don't you dare step one foot on it again." He couldn't see me, but I could surely hear him, and so could every other mother who was out to see her child off to school.

As sweetly as three-year-olds can talk, ours turned to this angry neighbor and said, "You can step on our lawn if you want to." The next day that neighbor came out with a big smile and a darling teddy bear, and he gave it to our little son. There was never again a problem over that lawn.

Sources and Permissions

Some of the short anecdotes included in boxes throughout the text were taken from

> Barbara B. Smith, *Growth in Grandmothering* (Salt Lake City: Bookcraft, 1986).

> *Best-Loved Humor of LDS People,* ed. Linda Ririe Gundry, Jay A. Perry, and Jack M Lyon (Salt Lake City: Deseret Book Company, 1999).

> Virginia H. Pearce, ed., *Glimpses into the Life and Heart of Marjorie Pay Hinckley* (Salt Lake City: Deseret Book Company, 1999).

Happiness and Humor

"Seven Little Boys," by Spencer W. Kimball, from *The Teachings of Spencer W. Kimball: Twelfth President of The Church of Jesus Christ of Latter-day Saints,* ed. Edward L. Kimball (Salt Lake City: Bookcraft, 1982), pp. 484–85.

"A Bad Day?" by Kenneth L. Harvey, from LDSWorld-Gems website (www.ldsworld.com).

"Four Friends," by Ashby Miner. Previously unpublished.

"Wrong, but Not Far Off," by Paul Bouchard, from LDSWorld-Gems website (www.ldsworld.com).

"Single White Male, Primary Teacher," by Michaelene P. Grassli, from *What I Have Learned from Children* (Salt Lake City: Deseret Book Company, 1993), pp. 58–59.

"Listening to the Bishop," by Jeff Schrade, from LDSWorld-Gems website (www.ldsworld.com).

"A Cure for Anger," by Linda J. Eyre, from *A Joyful Mother of Children: The Magic and Mayhem of Motherhood* (Salt Lake City: Deseret Book Company, 2000), p. 191.

"A Reverent Mouth," by Amy Menough, from the LDSWorld-Gems Website (www.ldsworld.com).

"'You Did Real Good, Honey,'" by Lynda Rae and Leonard Marden, from LDSWorld-Gems website (www.ldsworld.com).

"A Tough Interview with the Bishop," by Lois Carter, from the Deseret Book website (www.deseretbook.com).

"Two Kind Deeds?" by Michaelene P. Grassli, from *What I Have Learned from Children* (Salt Lake City: Deseret Book Company, 1993), pp. 50–51.

Family

"The Faith of a Little Child," by Tamra Christensen. Previously unpublished.

"The Upgrade," by Robert Farrell Smith. Previously unpublished.

"'Look Who's Here!'" by Barbara B. Smith, from "Roots and Wings," in *1978 Devotional Speeches of the Year* (Provo, Utah: Brigham Young University Press, 1979), pp. 14–15.

"Source of Income," by Shane Adamson. Previously unpublished.

"Two Fathers," by Eric Knight, from the LDSWorld-Gems website (www.ldsworld.com).

"Dad Can Fix It," by W. Timothy Hill, from the LDSWorld-Gems website (www.ldsworld.com).

"Little Arms of Comfort," by Lisa J. Peck. Previously unpublished.

"Family First," by Paul Cox, from the LDSWorld-Gems website (www.ldsworld.com).

"Sister Mom and Elder Dad," by Michaelene P. Grassli, from *What I Have Learned from Children* (Salt Lake City: Deseret Book Company, 1993), p. 15.

Scriptures

"'Peace, Be Still,'" by Kristen Hudson, from the LDSWorld-Gems website (www.ldsworld.com).

"Sacred Scrolls," by Mickie Mortensen Oritz, from the Deseret Book website (www.deseretbook.com).

"The Thirteenth Article of Faith," by Terry Alderman, from the LDSWorld-Gems website (www.ldsworld.com).

"The Book of Mormon and *The Cat in the Hat*," by Julie Sessions, from the LDSWorld-Gems website (www.ldsworld.com).

"'That's Not How It Goes!'" by Stefenee Hymas, from the LDSWorld-Gems website (www.ldsworld.com).

"Joshua and President Kimball," by Barbara B. Smith, from *Growth in Grandmothering* (Salt Lake City: Bookcraft, 1986), pp. 20–21.

"'Heinous, Heinous, Yay!'" by Kimberly Ottosen, from the LDSWorld-Gems website (www.ldsworld.com).

Holidays

"The Truth about the Easter Bunny," by Barbara B. Smith, from *Growth in Grandmothering* (Salt Lake City: Bookcraft, 1986), p. 111.

"The Anonymous Benefactor," by Susan Easton Black, from *Keeping Christmas: Stories from the Heart* (Salt Lake City: Deseret Book Company, 1996), pp. 12–17.

"Faith in Christ," by Mignon Coley, from the LDSWorld-Gems website (www.ldsworld.com).

"An Easter Egg Hunt," by L. E. Jacobsen. Previously unpublished.

"A Teacher's Christmas," by Brad Wilcox. Previously unpublished.

"A Magical Christmas," by Richard Peterson. Previously unpublished.

Heaven and Deity

"The Most Important Thing," by F. Enzio Busche, from *Friend* 10 (October 1980): 6–7.

"'More Room in Heaven,'" by Leslie Jensen, from the LDSWorld-Gems website (www.ldsworld.com).

"Heavenly Father Knows," author unknown, from Deseret Book website (www.deseretbook.com).

"A Young Admirer," by Peter B. Gardner. Previously unpublished.

"A Voice of Warning," by Harold B. Lee, from Jay A. Parry and others, eds. *Best-Loved Stories of the LDS People,* vol. 2 (Salt Lake City: Deseret Book Company, 1999), pp. 336–37.

"Which One Was He?" by Julie Steinberg, from the LDSWorld-Gems website (www.ldsworld.com).

"The Purity of a Child," by Dean Wessendorf, from the LDSWorld-Gems website (www.ldsworld.com).

"The Most Influential People," by Shonna C. Dodson, from the LDSWorld-Gems website (www.ldsworld.com).

"A Child's Testimony," by Shane Dixon. Previously unpublished.

"Words of Wisdom," by Monty Hays, from the LDSWorld-Gems website (www.ldsworld.com).

A Child's Perspective

"The Simple Pleasures of Childhood," by Janene Wolsey Baadsgaard, from *Families Who Laugh . . . Last* (Salt Lake City: Deseret Book Company, 1992), pp. 152–53.

"The Good Food," by Nona L. Brady, from the LDSWorld-Gems website (www.ldsworld.com).

"'Poor, Yet Possessing All Things,'" by Joyce Baggerly. Previously unpublished.

"Reverently, Quietly," by Susan A. Sandberg, from the LDSWorld-Gems website (www.ldsworld.com).

"'What Makes You Have a Bad Day?'" by Marsha Rose Steed, from the LDSWorld-Gems website (www.ldsworld.com).

"Blessings for Eva," by Peter B. Gardner. Previously unpublished.

"'My Body *Is* the Happy,'" by Linda J. and Richard Eyre, from *Teaching Children Joy* (Salt Lake City: Shadow Mountain, 1984), pp. 22–23.

"Authority to Baptize," by M. Katherine Edwards, from the LDSWorld-Gems Website (www.ldsworld.com).

"Spilt Milk," by Char Gwyn, from the LDSWorld-Gems website (www.ldsworld.com).

"The Grand Amen," by Valerie Buck. Previously unpublished.

Faith, Courage, and Determination

"'I Will Have My Father . . . Hold Me in His Arms,'" by Lucy Mack

Smith, from *Best-Loved Stories of the LDS People* (Salt Lake City: Deseret Book Company, 1997), pp. 178–81.

"Ballad of the Tempest," by James Thomas Fields, from *Best-Loved Poems of the LDS People* (Salt Lake City: Deseret Book Company, 1996), p. 82.

"Bricks or Straw?" by Ardeth Greene Kapp, from *Miracles in Pinafores and Bluejeans* (Salt Lake City: Deseret Book Company, 1977), 75–76.

"'What if You Die, Mom?'" by Daniel Quillen, from the LDSWorld-Gems website (www.ldsworld.com).

"'Throw It Here, Sissy!'" by Heber J. Grant, from *Best-Loved Stories of the LDS People* (Salt Lake City: Deseret Book Company, 1997), pp. 157–58.

"'He Blessed Me That I Might Be Healed,'" by George Albert Smith, from *Best-Loved Stories of the LDS People* (Salt Lake City: Deseret Book Company, 1997), pp. 350–51.

"Fasting for Grandma," by Wilma Aebischer, from the LDSWorld-Gems website (www.ldsworld.com).

"Saving the Book of Commandments," by Mary Elizabeth Rollins Lightner, from *Best-Loved Stories of the LDS People* (Salt Lake City: Deseret Book Company, 1997), pp. 191–92.

Gospel Principles

"The Building Fund Goat," by Eldon Ross Palmer. Previously unpublished.

"Wash Away Sins," by Kent Stephens, from the LDSWorld-Gems website (www.ldsworld.com).

"It's Sometimes Hard to Say No," by Stephanie Jenson, from the LDSWorld-Gems website (www.ldsworld.com).

"Heidi Loves the Sacrament," by Beckie W. Kearl, adapted from *Friend* 26 (September 1996): 34–35.

"I'll Soon Be Eight," by Geneva Facemyer. Previously unpublished.

"I Love to See the Temple," by Fiona Howell, from the LDSWorld-Gems website (www.ldsworld.com).

"The Confession," by Mel Jones, from the LDSWorld-Gems website (www.ldsworld.com).

"'You Don't Have the Priesthood (Yet),'" by Yolanda Dixon. Previously unpublished.

"Giving Credit Where Credit Is Due," by Marsha Hughes, from Deseret Book website (www.deseretbook.com).

Birth, Death, and Resurrection

"To Live with Father in Heaven," by Rod Boss, from the LDSWorld-Gems website (www.ldsworld.com).

"Born Here," by Brad Wilcox. Previously unpublished.

"Repairing Grandpa," by Robert P. Barnes, from the LDSWorld-Gems website (www.ldsworld.com).

"The Age of a Tree," by Lori Smith, from the LDSWorld-Gems website (www.ldsworld.com).

"Burying Fred," by Elyssa Renee Andrus. Previously unpublished.

"A Potato Bug Reunion," by Michaelene P. Grassli, from *What I Have Learned from Children* (Salt Lake City: Deseret Book Company, 1993), pp. 83–84.

"Simple Faith," by Juliann Doman. Previously unpublished.

"The Will of the Lord," by Marba C. Josephson, from *Best-Loved Stories of the LDS People,* ed. Jack M. Lyon and others (Salt Lake City: Deseret Book Company, 1997), p. 267.

Prayer

"'Nothing Will Hurt You,'" by David O. McKay, from *Best-Loved Stories of the LDS People,* ed. Jack M. Lyon and others (Salt Lake City: Deseret Book Company, 1997), pp. 274–75.

"An Unusual Answer," by Linda Tenney. Previously unpublished.

"'How About Your Prayers,'" by Robert L. Simpson, from *Best-Loved Stories of the LDS People* vol. 2, ed. Jay A. Parry and others (Salt Lake City: Deseret Book Company, 1999), p. 295.

"'Doctor, Won't You Pray for Me?'" by George Albert Smith, from *Best-Loved Stories of the LDS People* vol. 2, ed. Jay A. Parry and others (Salt Lake City: Deseret Book Company, 1999), pp. 88–89.

"'But What Should I Say, Daddy?'" by Ron Mathes, from Deseret Book website (www.deseretbook.com).

"'For Such Is the Kingdom of God,'" by Cindy Collyer, from the LDSWorld-Gems website (www.ldsworld.com).

"A Prayer for Bobby," by Michaelene P. Grassli, from *What I Have Learned from Children* (Salt Lake City: Deseret Book Company, 1993), p. 48.

"'And Please Bless . . . ,'" by Matthew O. Richardson. Previously unpublished.

"A Sister in a Storm," by Kathy Ford, from the LDSWorld-Gems website (www.ldsworld.com).

"Michael's Prayer," by Michaelene P. Grassli, from *What I Have Learned from Children* (Salt Lake City: Deseret Book Company, 1993), pp. 24–25.

"'The Wind Has Gone Down!'" Sophy H. Valentine, from *Best-Loved Stories of the LDS People* vol. 2, ed. Jay A. Parry and others (Salt Lake City: Deseret Book Company, 1999), pp. 89–91.

"Faith of a Child," by Heber C. Kimball, from *Best-Loved Stories of the LDS People,* ed. Jack M. Lyon and others (Salt Lake City: Deseret Book Company, 1997), p. 133.

Love and Service

"Love Thy Neighbor," by Ardeth Greene Kapp, from *Best-Loved Humor of LDS People,* ed. Linda Ririe Gundry, Jay A. Perry, and Jack M Lyon (Salt Lake City: Deseret Book Company, 1999), 234–35.

"'I Didn't Want You to Be Alone,'" by Michaelene P. Grassli, from *What I Have Learned from Children* (Salt Lake City: Deseret Book Company, 1993), pp. 57–58.

"'Daddy, Why Do You Love Me?'" by Scott Satterfield, from the LDSWorld-Gems website (www.ldsworld.com).

"Angels in Camouflage," by Corina Burner, from the LDSWorld-Gems website (www.ldsworld.com).

"'Because He Loved Them,'" by Shane Dixon. Previously unpublished.

"Pacified," by Linda J. Eyre, from *A Joyful Mother of Children: The Magic and Mayhem of Motherhood* (Salt Lake City: Shadow Mountain, 2000), p. 34.

"The Mean Man Next Door," by Angie Olson, from the LDSWorld-Gems website (www.ldsworld.com).

"Friends for Andre," by Michaelene P. Grassli, from *What I Have Learned from Children* (Salt Lake City: Deseret Book Company, 1993), pp. 47–48.

"Ears to Hear," by Paula Hunt. Previously unpublished.

"A Turf War Averted," by Barbara B. Smith, from "Love Is Life, and Life Hath Immortality," *Brigham Young University 1983–84 Fireside and Devotional Speeches* (Provo, Utah: University Communications, 1984), p. 70.